LIFESAVERS OF
THE SOUTH SHORE

LIFESAVERS OF THE SOUTH SHORE

A HISTORY OF RESCUE AND LOSS

JOHN GALLUZZO
FOREWORD BY RALPH SHANKS

Charleston   London

THE
History
PRESS

Published by The History Press
Charleston, SC 29403
www.historypress.net

Copyright © 2008 by John Galluzzo
All rights reserved

Cover design by Marshall Hudson.

First published 2008

Manufactured in the United Kingdom

ISBN 978.1.59629.224.6

Library of Congress Cataloging-in-Publication Data

Galluzzo, John.
Lifesavers of the South Shore : a history of rescue and loss / John Galluzzo.
p. cm.
Includes bibliographical references.
ISBN 978-1-59629-224-6
1. Lifesaving--Massachusetts--History. 2. Lifesaving stations--Massachusetts--History. 3. United States.
Life-Saving Service--History. 4. Shipwrecks--Massachusetts. 5. Rescues--Massachusetts. I. Title.
VK1324.M4G35 2008
363.286--dc22
                                      2008013256

To Ava Victoria. This is just the first of several stories I plan to tell you in your life.

CONTENTS

FOREWORD

The first maritime rescue organizations in the world were established in China. The first in America was in Massachusetts. This says a great deal about the people of both places, for until comparatively late times Massachusetts, China and several European countries were the only locations in the world where mariners could count on organized rescue work. The concept of saving the lives of complete strangers from the perils of the sea was not widespread until recent times.

In America, the Massachusetts Humane Society, an organization created to save human lives rather than animals, led the way. By the 1870s the United States Life-Saving Service was formed as an agency of the federal government. Both organizations operated rescue stations and boats in Massachusetts and achieved remarkable records of bravery at sea. The Life-Saving Service eventually became the U.S. Coast Guard and courageous search and rescue work continues along the Massachusetts coast to this day.

Why focus specifically on the South Shore of Massachusetts Bay? The reasons are many and important. The first lifesaving station in America was established here at Cohasset. The most famous maritime rescuer in American history, Joshua James, called Hull home. Most of the fascinating rescues involving both the U.S. Life-Saving Service and the Massachusetts Humane Society occurred along the South Shore. The treacherous weather of this dangerous coast combined to produce not just one, but sometimes numerous shipwrecks in a single day!

We cannot fully understand American maritime history without knowing the story of the South Shore. We cannot really comprehend this region's history without meeting the surfmen who were the rescuers here. Imagine facing hurricane-force winds and breaking seas and yet unhesitatingly going to the aid of all who were in danger. This was what the surfmen stood ready to do each day and each night.

Historian, naturalist, author and editor John Galluzzo is well qualified to tell this remarkable tale. John is a native of the South Shore. It is truly his home port. He has spent his life studying and writing about this great coast. John has also dedicated himself to preserving the rich heritage of the surfmen, their families, their stations, their boats and equipment. Join him now as he takes you on a fascinating maritime adventure along this amazing shore. Put on your life jacket, dress warmly and hold on tight. It will be quite a ride when his surfboat shoves off from the breach.

Ralph Shanks, MA
Maritime Historian and Anthropologist
Novato, California
Author, *The United States Life-Saving Service: Heroes, Rescues and Architecture of the Early Coast Guard*

ACKNOWLEDGEMENTS

When you grow up in Hull, Massachusetts, you're barely able to walk and talk before you learn about the local hero, Joshua James. When you become a Coast Guard historian and travel the United States visiting active units on the East Coast, West Coast, Gulf Coast and Great Lakes, you find that those people who introduced you to Joshua James weren't kidding: his countenance is found in Coast Guard stations everywhere.

Before I was born, there were people who worked to unbury the Joshua James story, a tale lost in the shuffle of two World Wars, the Great Depression and subsequent American transience. While the old-time families of Hull—the Mitchells, Cleverlys, Jameses (through their descendants the Means and Goulart families) and Popes, among others—have always remembered the deeds of Hull's lifesavers, the greater town had all but forgotten their stories of heroism and sacrifice. The recently departed Ken Black, commanding the Point Allerton Coast Guard Station in the 1960s (then still in the same building Joshua James had used in the 1890s), led the resurgence, decorating the grave of the old keeper. William M. "Doc" Bergan, author of the most important book ever written on Hull history, *Old Nantasket*, dedicated precious space in his book to the Joshua James story. Thanks to their efforts, new generations of Hullonians have been introduced to an important old story.

I met Judeth Van Hamm when I was just an elementary school student, back when she was Judy Wiers. Judeth and Ed McCabe came into our sixth-grade classroom to talk about a new venture that was just getting off the ground: the Hull Lifesaving Museum. That summer, while standing on a Civil War battlefield in Kentucky, the history bug bit me for good (I just hope it wasn't a tick, actually), and I started to read history books in earnest.

The history of the Coast Guard, though, would have to wait until after I received my history degree from the University of Massachusetts at Amherst in 1993. I spent two years working out of town after graduation before returning home in 1995 and then, armed with skills honed by four years of intensive history research and writing, I began to turn over stones in my hometown. I wandered into the Hull Lifesaving Museum and started to simply hang out there, fascinated with the stories of bravery and selflessness of the old lifesavers. In 1996, I began leading tours at the station as a volunteer, working side by side with the museum's number one docent, Captain Bob Dever, himself the son of a lifesaver who had worked at the City Point floating station in Dorchester. When the spring of 1996 rolled around, I became sick to my stomach at the thought of returning to a full-time landscaping job, and accepted a $2,000 pay cut—from $16,000 annually to $14,000—to work as an educator at the museum. For the next four years I was proud to work with the regular staff, including director Lory Newmyer, Ed McCabe, the now departed and deeply missed Barbie Guild, curator Paula Kozol, Corinne Leung, boatbuilder Reuben Smith, fellow educator Corie Fehsenfeld, gift shop managers Beth Myers-West and Al Almeida and the many Hull kids who worked summers at the museum. In all, I estimate that three thousand kids rode the breeches buoy across the street from the museum while I was at the museum, and my hands had the rope burns every spring and summer to prove it. I'm sure the staff will not be upset when I say that I learned as much from the kids as I did from everybody else.

The Hull story does not end with the Hull Lifesaving Museum, though. Richard Cleverly, our town historian, opened the doors of the Hull Historical Society and helped me see how lifesaving fit into the greater context of the history of the town. Numerous other historians in town, including Chris Haraden, who introduced me to his copy of *Old Nantasket* at twelve years old, and Dan Johnson, director of the Hull Public Library, have helped me in the search for Hull's stories of lifesaving. Several of the stories that appear in this book first appeared in slightly different formats in the *Hull Times*, encouraged by my adopted work mom, Susan Ovans. I owe Susan and her husband Roger Jackson a huge debt of gratitude for allowing me to cut my writing teeth on their beloved weekly.

My adventures in lifesaving history headed south from there, to the Scituate Historical Society, where in particular I worked with David Ball, Fred Freitas, Carol and Paul Miles, David Corbin and so many others in telling the tales of the lifesavers of that community. In Marshfield, I've been lucky and privileged to work with the town historian, Cynthia Krusell.

In 1997, I attended the third annual meeting of the United States Life-Saving Service Heritage Association and began forging friendships with colleagues that have lasted now for more than a decade. Through the organization I've come to know Maurice Gibbs and Jeremy Slavitz of Nantucket; Ralph Shanks of Novato, California; Fred Stonehouse of Marquette, Michigan; Dennis Noble of Sequim, Washington; Robert Browning and Scott Price of the Coast Guard Historian's Office; the late Van R. Field of Center Moriches, New York; Jeff Shook of Fenton, Michigan; Richard Ryder of Eastham and William P. Quinn of Orleans, Massachusetts; Dave Pinyerd of Albany, Oregon; Drew Loizeaux of Anna Maria, Florida; Kim Mann and Bill Herd of the Sleeping Bear Dunes National Lakeshore in Michigan; Bob Trapani, now the director of the American Lighthouse Foundation in Maine; Wick York of Stonington, Connecticut; Jerry Ostermiller, director of the Columbia River Maritime Museum; Fred "Bud" Cooney of Charlestown, Rhode Island; the late Dr. R.W. Haley of West Roxbury and

Hull, Massachusetts; and many, many, *many* more. I'd need another book to list the names of every person with whom I have shared history moments pertaining to the Life-Saving Service story.

While the Coast Guard has been maligned in the past—including by me—for not taking care of its history, there are certainly individuals and units that do their best to keep local traditions alive. I know I'm just a civilian, but I salute Chief Warrant Officer Craig Bitler, Senior Chief Boatswain's Mate Bruce Bradley, Chief Warrant Officer Patrick Higgins, Chief Boatswain's Mate Rick Barone, Chief Warrant Officer Paul Sordillo, Chief Boatswain's Mate Jim Bodenrader, Captain Dana Goward, Chief Warrant Officer Tom Guthlein (who even named his son Joshua James) and all the others around the country I've met for all they've done to keep their service's history alive. I'd especially like to thank Senior Chief Boatswain's Mate David Considine and Captain W. Russell Webster for their camaraderie, and Chief Warrant Officer Bernie Webber for helping me understand the true meaning of humility.

In recent years, I've had the privilege of doing some volunteer work for the Foundation for Coast Guard History, and have learned much about life in the service from friends Admiral Howard Thorsen, Captain Robert L. Desh, Captain Fred Herzberg, Captain Barrett Tom Beard, Chief Warrant Officer Sandy Schwaab and more. Internationally, I'd like to thank Canada's greatest Coast Guardsmen, Ed Greer and Inga Thorsteinson, and Great Britain's leading lifeboat historian, Nicholas Leach.

Increasingly over the past year, Dr. William Thiesen, the Coast Guard's Atlantic area historian, has become someone with whom I can brainstorm about the service's history and what can be done to preserve it. His inspiration deserves special mention.

While working on this book, I've been simultaneously tackling a separate project with the Humane Society of the Commonwealth of Massachusetts, and would like to thank Trustees Dr. Curtis Prout and Lawrence Perera for their guidance and patience, and Beth Nilsson for all her help.

My family has never wavered in supporting my dream of researching history, so to my father Bob, mother Marylou, sister Julie and brother Nick, thank you. My wife, Michelle, has given me the space I've needed to make this project come together, and for that I am eternally grateful. And I'm now a godfather twice over, thanks to the birth of Nick's daughter Ava Victoria.

Two special educators—R. Dean Ware and the late Franklin Wickwire—pointed me down the right path while I studied history at the University of Massachusetts at Amherst, and a special group of friends that go all the way back to that time—David and Kathy Dean, Jay and Leah Kennan, Rich and Felice Eby and Fred Hoth—still make me smile to this day. And now, a decade and a half beyond graduation, I am gaining new friends at the UMass History Department—Julia Sandy-Bailey and Professor Anne Broadbridge—and the many history majors I've had the pleasure to meet in recent trips "back home."

George Kerr is forever in my thoughts, and will be mentioned in every book I write for the rest of my life. Go Sox, go Curt, go Papa G!

Joanie Gearin at the National Archives and Records Administration branch in Waltham, Massachusetts, has been everything we hope our federal employees would be and more: efficient, thoughtful, patient and ready to help at a moment's notice. My coauthor Don Cann has joined me on most of my trips to the NARA and patiently waited for me to finish the project so we can tackle our next one together.

Finally, the glue that held this entire project together was Dick Boonisar. I met Dick at that 1997 meeting at the Coffin School on Nantucket, when he was stepping down as president of the U.S. Life-Saving Service Heritage Association. I've had the privilege of doing research on his behalf in England, touring his privately owned lifesaving station on several occasions and delving into countless conversations with him about the minutiae of Life-Saving Service, Revenue Cutter Service, Coast Guard and Humane Society history. Each time I have come away wiser and more amazed at the depth and breadth of his knowledge. This book happened because I know Dick Boonisar.

Any errors fall squarely on my shoulders. Blame me, not them.

INTRODUCTION

They were called storm fighters and storm warriors. When wind and wave conspired to kill those who dared to tread upon the sea, the men of the United States Life-Saving Service left the comfort of their sturdy stations and entered the battle. With nothing more than wooden boats, cork life jackets and the oilskin foul weather gear on their backs, they let their muscle, determination and bravery lead the way. Time and again they smirked in the face of danger and stole back the lives of men who were supposed to be dead, victims intended to be claimed by shipwrecks caused by storms.

While the birth of the Life-Saving Service took place elsewhere, the South Shore of Boston is where the first lifeboat ever intended for launching from the shore to a wreck on the American coast was placed. For before there was the United States Life-Saving Service, there was the Humane Society of the Commonwealth of Massachusetts. Volunteers who worked their boats during times of disaster lived by the motto, "I'd like to think that if I was the one out there, someone would come for me."

The Life-Saving Service attempted to take the Humane Society model of volunteer crews to the New Jersey and Long Island shorelines, but it simply didn't work. It took the efficiency and drive of a new director of the Revenue Marine Bureau, Maine-bred Sumner Increase Kimball, to invigorate the system of lifesaving stations along those coasts and expand it around the country. In 1874, he brought the Life-Saving Service to the South Shore, ordering the construction of two Plymouth stations. By 1893, six stations stood guard along the South Shore from Plymouth to Hull.

Local boys grew up saving lives with the Humane Society, and died as Life-Saving Service and Coast Guard heroes. Some gained national recognition, while others toiled in relative obscurity. Too many died in the course of their duty. Around the United States, the Life-Saving Service saved 186,000 lives from shipwreck between 1878 and 1915, with many of those rescues taking place on the approach to Boston.

In 1915, the United States Life-Saving Service merged with the Revenue Cutter Service to form the Coast Guard. Technologies changed. Better means of communication and self-powered lifeboats obviated the need for men walking beaches with kerosene lanterns. The Coast Guard decommissioned stations and left them empty. Some ended up in private hands; others fell to the wrecking ball. Three of the six stand today, and the South Shore boasts one of the finest lifesaving museums in the United States, in Hull.

This book is about the men of the South Shore and their legendary deeds, of Fred Stanley, Benjamin Manter, George H. Brown and certainly Joshua James. Years after the Life-Saving Service was gone, a Coast Guard magazine article attributed a saying to a Life-Saving Service keeper that may or may not have been said by him. When asked about heading seaward during a particularly terrible gale, the keeper said, "The regulations say we have to go out; they say nothing about coming back."

Spoken or not, these are the words the surfmen and keepers of the Life-Saving Service lived by. This is their story.

ULRICA

At 8:00 a.m. on December 16, 1896, Keeper Joshua James of the United States Life-Saving Service's station at Point Allerton in Hull had a decision to make. For the past day and a half the barometric pressure had steadily been dropping, from 30.17 at midnight on December 15, to 30.11, to 29.90, to 29.70 at sunrise that morning. The temperature bottomed out at that time, too, at 26 degrees, and the seas had gone from serene and smooth to ugly and rough over the same period. Northeast winds had been blowing for twenty-four hours, increasing until James felt a proper gale was blowing. And by sunrise on the December 16, snow had arrived.

Surfman Martin Quinn returned from the station's west patrol at eight that morning, having left at four. Surfman Louis Galiano trudged in from the south beat. Both shook themselves free of the snow that had assaulted them on their walks, and both reported to their captain the same news: there was no news.

Quinn took a moment to refresh and then climbed the ladder to the cupola, assigned the day watch. James checked the patrol list of the past night and picked two names, James Murphy and Francis Mitchell, for extra duty. Although the surfmen normally patrolled only at night, the reduced visibility forced the keeper's hand. He sent Murphy on the south patrol, eastward to Point Allerton and thence southward on Nantasket Beach, and Mitchell to the west, toward Pemberton Point.

Before the hour was out, a phone message came in from George Hatchard, a resident living to the south. A ship, a three-masted vessel of some kind, had come ashore and was being pounded by the breakers. By the time the message reached the station at 8:45 a.m., Surfman Murphy had spotted the ship as well and started running to tell the rest of the crew. Along the way he took the initiative of engaging resident C.M. Clemmons and a team of horses to go down the beach and retrieve the Humane Society's big lifeboat, *Nantasket*, the favored rescue craft of the keeper, to the beach to await the arrival of the crew. As Clemmons headed south, Murphy pushed on to the station through the elements.

Before the surfman could reach the station, though, James Jeffries of the New York, New Haven & Hartford Railroad offered Keeper James and his men the services of the

Above: The schooner *Ulrica* put the men of the Point Allerton Life-Saving Station to the test on December 16, 1896. *Courtesy of the Hull Historical Society.*

Left: Joshua James, the keeper of the Point Allerton Life-Saving Station, is recognized as the "Father of the Coast Guard" for his six decades of lifesaving service. *Courtesy of the United States Coast Guard.*

railroad's cars. James arranged for John L. Mitchell, from the nearby village, to transport the station's beach apparatus cart down the beach while he and his men boarded the train. They arrived simultaneously with Clemmons and his horses and joined the man in collecting the lifeboat, which together they brought to the scene of the wreck.

With the ship in the breakers, standard procedure called for the rigging of the beach apparatus, firing a line-throwing gun to carry a rope to the vessel that would start the construction of a rope bridge from ship to shore. But with a heavy sea running and the lives of the men aboard clearly in momentous peril, James decided he could not wait for John Mitchell to arrive. He sent Clemmons farther down the beach to retrieve the Humane Society's gear from the mortar station and prepared his men to launch *Nantasket*.

Even in the snow, a small crowd had gathered on the beach. Surfman Francis Mitchell, on the west patrol, was unaware of what was unfolding on Nantasket Beach, and thus the crew was short-handed by one man. James called for six volunteers, who readily stepped forward. Brothers Joseph T. and Alfred A. Galiano, Alonzo Lovell Mitchell, Ambrose Burnside Mitchell, Benjamin Franklin Pope and James F. Dowd, all storm-tested surf warriors, quickly moved to join the station's crew, which consisted of Keeper James, Murphy, Quinn, Matthew Hoar, George F. Pope and Joseph and Alfred Galiano's brother Louis, in the lifeboat.

The ship sat just over a thousand feet from shore. With the keeper at the steering oar, the *Nantasket*'s crew pulled with all their might, endeavoring to reach the wreck. About halfway to the ship, they ran into a powerful current, slowing their progress. Suddenly, a wave overtook the boat and drove it backward. The steering oar, protruding from the stern of the vessel, by the force of the movement stood straight upward and flipped Keeper James into the frigid, churning water. The seventy-year-old reached out and grasped one of the surfmen's oars, holding on as the waves swept the boat back to the beach.

In the meantime, John L. Mitchell had arrived with the station's beach cart. By now the sea had taken vicious steps toward the ship's destruction. With the vessel lying nearly broadside to the beach, with its bow pointing slightly offshore, water had broken over the vessel from the mizzenmast forward, leaving the cabin on the aft deck as the only dry spot on the ship. Some of the men on the ship did not trust the sea to not take that as well, so they climbed the mizzen rigging.

James aimed his Lyle line-throwing gun for that section of the ship. His first shot landed on the mizzen topmast, but the crew made no attempt to retrieve it. The second landed above the mizzen crosstree on the topmast, a perfect place for it, but under the circumstances it was out of the reach of the crew. The third shot struck the side of the rigging and slid down toward the deck, within reachable distance of the crew. Ashore, the lifesavers, now joined by another volunteer, George Lowe, tied a whip line onto the thin shot line and motioned for the ship's crew to haul away. The current dragged the line sideways and floating wreckage impaired the process, but slowly the whip made its way to the ship. The hawser, the heaviest line and the one on which the breeches buoy would ride, was hauled off next.

From shore, James could see that the exhausted men on the ship could not climb the rigging high enough to properly rig the breeches buoy. He envisioned tangled lines and men being dragged through the roiling water and debris, a process more dangerous than lifesaving. Although their first attempt had failed, James thought the best course of action would be to try the lifeboat for a second go, as time was running out for the stranded sailors.

The station's crew took five volunteers with them this time, leaving others behind on the beach to man the hawser stretching from ship to shore. As they launched, the boat crew took several heavy seas broadside, blasts of green water that exploded off the lifeboat. Using the hawser as a guide and the oars for propulsion, with some men in the boat pulling hand over hand on the rope, the lifeboat crew persistently drove onward, the men ashore holding the hawser on a steady course to the ship. Reaching the vessel, the lifesavers found the men "in a benumbed exhausted condition and unable to help themselves." They climbed aboard the vessel and helped the sailors into the lifeboat before turning for home. The return trip was anticlimactic. The lifeboat crew landed safely ashore at 12:30 p.m.

With the survivors in a terrible state, nearly frozen to their cores, James knew the trip back to the lifesaving station by carriage through the storm, with the snow now increasing in thickness, could prove detrimental, if not murderous. Another bystander resident, Charles Jones, offered yet another team of horses, and he took six of the men to John R. Spearwater's Sea Foam House, a local hotel, on the bayside of A Street. One man, in the worst condition of all, could not take even that journey, and was transported to the nearest available shelter, the home of a Mr. Farrell.

James and the station's crew headed for the Sea Foam House to begin the warming process for the sailors, stripping them of their wet clothes and rubbing their muscles to stimulate them into movement. Mr. Spearwater rushed through the hotel collecting blankets and boiling water for coffee. The lifesavers took note of patches of slight frostbite on the faces of several of the men, and discovered that the ship's captain had one hand badly frozen. C.M. Clemmons headed for the lifesaving station to gather clothing from the trunk supplied by the Women's National Relief Association and more blankets to wrap the sailors in for their ride to the building. Half of the lifesaving crew returned to the beach to collect their lifesaving equipment, while the other half stuck close to the shipwreck survivors. The keeper took note of the name of the ship, the *Ulrica*, and guessed it would be a total loss.

The lifesavers reached the station at 4:00 p.m., and with the sun going down, James ordered his men back out on patrol for the night. Such was a day in the life of the Life-Saving Service.

THE HUMANE SOCIETY
OF THE COMMONWEALTH
OF MASSACHUSETTS

Boston is the birthplace of organized shore-based lifesaving of mariners in distress at sea in the United States. The Humane Society of the Commonwealth of Massachusetts, formed in the mid-1780s, raised the funds and awareness necessary for a young nation to take its first steps toward a proactive system of volunteer-manned lifeboats and mortar stations. The society, incorporated by the state of Massachusetts in 1791, put its theories on lifesaving into practical testing on the South Shore.

The American Revolution had hardly ended when a blind Scottish physician named Dr. Henry Moyes arrived in the new United States to begin a speaking tour. According to author John Anthony Harrison,

> *Moyes landed in Boston in May 1784 and made the town his headquarters for his projected lecture tour. His educational invasion had begun. The new republic accepted Moyes with open arms; indeed, he must have been the first lecturer to cross the Atlantic for many years. A course quickly started in Boston ran to a successful conclusion. Culture-starved Bostonians were quick to respond to this popular form of adult education and pressed Moyes to deliver another course in the town. But he had planned the tour carefully and had drawn up a schedule of lectures which he meant to keep. The Bostonians were firmly, but politely, told to wait.*

Although nominally no longer enemies with the Americans, having signed the Treaty of Paris opposite the signatures of John Jay, Benjamin Franklin and John Adams, the British nonetheless encouraged others to take the fight to their former colony. Concomitantly, though, the former colonial ruler recognized the potential for trade with the young country. The Treaty of Paris was ratified by the American Congress in January 1784; later in the year the first bales of American cotton reached England.

For more than a year, Moyes lectured around the United States on topics such as "heat," "air" and "vegetable substances." He finally returned to Boston in November 1785, welcomed by a crowd of listeners eager to learn. One quiet winter's evening

Early Humane Society lifeboat stations, like this one on Tuckernuck Island off Nantucket, simply served to store lifeboats and equipment. *Courtesy of the Nantucket Life-Saving Museum.*

By the middle of the nineteenth century, the Humane Society's volunteer lifesavers had become nationally renowned for their boat handling prowess. In this picture of the Hull volunteers, Joshua James is peeking over the shoulder of another man at the stern. Joshua's older brother Samuel designed the boat. *Courtesy of the Hull Historical Society.*

he shared the story of the formation of an organization in England dedicated to the restoration of the "apparently drowned," known as a "Humane Society." His words sparked interest. The next night, one of the men sharing in his conversation produced a Royal Humane Society pamphlet that he had seen somewhere in the city. Three men— Reverend James Freeman, Dr. Aaron Dexter and Royall Tyler, Esquire—transcribed the regulations of the British organization and made changes that better suited life in the United States. Word spread throughout the streets of a potential new endeavor, a Humane Society of the Commonwealth of Massachusetts.

On January 5, 1786, citizens convinced to subscribe to the cause met at the Bunch of Grapes Tavern on the corner of King Street and Mackerel Lane to carry the idea forward. Edwin Lassetter Bynner wrote in 1889,

> *On a certain fair day, or it may have been night, in 1785 [sic], there was born in the old inn, not a babe, but a project, which must by no means be forgotten, for it had as sponsors James Bowdoin, Rev. James Freeman, and other noted men, and was destined to make a little stir in the world. Let there be no regret that it was not a veritable flesh-and-blood babe, for no human suckling known to our annals ever grew up to be such a power for good in the community as the Boston Humane Society.*

By the time of the meeting, Dr. Moyes had left for Philadelphia and another round of lectures.

From the meeting came a pamphlet that outlined the purpose of the new society and presented its case to the people of Boston:

> *From a variety of faithful experiments, and incontestable facts, it is now considered as an established truth, that the total suspension of the vital functions of the animal body is by no means incompatible with life; and consequently, the marks of apparent death may subsist without any necessary implication of an absolute extinction of the animating principle.*
>
> *The boundary line between life and death, or the distinguishing signs of the latter, are objects to which the utmost efforts of the human capacity have never yet attained. Nor can we, with any degree of certainty, pronounce, that an animal is dead, until the most unequivocal proofs of putrefaction have been furnished.*
>
> *From these facts it might reasonably be expected, that were proper measures to be adopted, especially in cases peculiarly doubtful, we might frequently be enabled to restore to full life, and the enjoyment of it, a beloved friend, or a valuable member of society. And indeed, numerous successful instances might be adduced in the cases of persons, who would in a few hours have been consigned to an untimely grave; and perhaps have suffered all the horrors of inevitable death, attended with a consciousness of their own terrible situation…*
>
> *Upon these considerations, societies have been formed in various parts of Europe for promoting attempts to recover persons from apparent death, especially in cases of suffocation and drowning. The Humane Society established in Great-Britain, in 1774,*

After a wreck, or a drill, as it appears in this case, the Humane Society's volunteers returned to their boathouse to recoil the line that had played out in firing their line-throwing gun. *Courtesy of Richard Boonisar.*

has been very successful. Within ten years from its institution, out of 1300 persons apparently dead from drowning, 790 have been restored to their friends and country. Many of them, no doubt, useful and valuable men.

For an institution of this nature a considerable fund is necessary. A proper apparatus must be procured. And many occasional expences will unavoidably occur. The cause of humanity, however, deserves every encouragement. And to promote that cause, it is to be hoped the benevolent will liberally subscribe.

The trustees of the new society held out hope that witnesses of tragedies that struck ordinary unsuspecting citizens would be willing to do their best to save their fellow men. And, according to their regulations, the trustees were willing to reward those men and women who did: "The person who shall first discover, and endeavour to recover the subject, shall be entitled to receive from the Treasurer of the Society, a sum not exceeding forty-eight shillings, nor less than six shillings, lawful money, at the discretion of the Trustees." More money awaited those heroes who took their bravery and cool-headedness to the utmost degree, offering thirty shillings to those "who shall, by signal exertion, save another from death."

The pamphlet was a first, important step, but a more imperative plan of action soon arose. While printed dissertations on how to preserve life after perceived drowning, not to mention "hanging, convulsion, fits, cold, suffocation by damps, or noxious vapors,

Around the beginning of the twentieth century, the keepers of the Humane Society's volunteer lifeboats in towns along the Massachusetts coast gathered to share their knowledge and experiences. Here, at a meeting in Hull, a breeches buoy demonstration takes place on Hull Hill. Peddocks Island is in the background to the left and the Pemberton Hotel is to the right. The Massachusetts Yacht Club is at the end of the pier. *Courtesy of the Hull Historical Society.*

the confined air of wells, cisterns, caves, or the must of fermenting liquors," supplied the necessary knowledge, providing the tools to enact those rescues became of supreme significance to the society.

Just a year after the society's formation, they took their cause to the coast. In 1787, the society erected three huts of refuge, two on South Shore beaches and one on Lovell's Island in Boston Harbor. That the society should equate the saving of lives so heavily with maritime dangers proves the importance of seagoing commerce to the new nation.

The society listed the first hut of refuge as being on "Scituate Beach," or about a mile south of the Fourth Cliff headland on the Humarock peninsula. The hut sat on the eastern shore of the peninsula, which at that time reached southward to the opening of the North River mouth near today's Rexhame Beach, and mirrored the ancient White's Ferry site on the river side. The choice of the Humarock site, while not caring for the obvious need of protecting either Plymouth or Boston Harbors, did provide relief for mariners either launching new ships from the North River or carrying goods to or from the various packet landings upriver. Although not a major port, the mouth of the river was certainly an active marine traffic center.

The second hut sat south of Point Allerton in Hull, the first prominent headland spotted by mariners turning inside Cape Cod and heading for the port of Boston. Good northeast winds could, and had, sent ships ashore to the south of the headland onto the three and a half miles of sandy Nantasket Beach. The hut of refuge allowed for the mariner to find temporary shelter while the residents of Hull Village, then just 125 strong, fought their way through the storm to help them.

The third hut, placed on the west end of Lovell's Island, marked a halfway point for ships entering Boston Harbor. After clearing Point Allerton, entering Lighthouse Channel, passing the outer harbor islands named for Elder William Brewster of Pilgrim fame and steering clear of a long, sandy spit coming off the largest of those islands, ships entered the Narrows, the northwesterly passage between Gallops, George's and Lovell's Islands. The western shore of the island marked the eastern side of the inbound and outbound passages. More importantly, the siting of the hut on that spot placed it centrally between the three islands, allowing notionally easy access for sailors wrecked on any one of them. The society built three more huts in 1789: one more on Nantasket Beach across from Strawberry Hill, another on Lovell's Island and one on Calf Island.

The future of lifesaving on the South Shore soon became evident, though, as the barrenness of the huts of refuge led to their unauthorized and abusive use by duck hunters and others who utilized the supplies inside for their own selfish purposes. An anonymous writer narrated a tale of two shipwrecked sailors in Hull in November 1794, in a letter published in the *Columbian Centinel* on April 11, 1795. A ship sailing from Cape Ann had driven ashore on the point, and its two sailors "with much difficulty swam, or otherwise got on shore; when, arrived at the asylum erected by humanity, they were disappointed of relief, the tinder box being wet, and otherwise in a situation useless to them; the provisions devoured by the mice, or some inhuman mouse in the shape of a man." Disoriented, cold, hungry and tired, the two men stumbled out onto the beach, where, by chance, they met a duck hunter preparing for the day's shoot on the plains of the peninsula. The hunter led them to safe lodging well down the beach. The anonymous well-wisher suggested that paid guardians be hired to watch over the buildings, especially during times of inclement weather. This arrangement would eventually come to pass with the creation of professionally staffed lifeboat stations operated by the United States Life-Saving Service, but that accomplishment loomed foggily decades into the future.

A second incident, also in Hull, on December 15, 1802, pushed the idea of manned lifesaving stations even further into the thinking of the trustees of the Humane Society. The brigantine *Elizabeth* had taken on a pilot in Lighthouse Channel with the hope of reaching Boston, but, already in bad condition, the ship faced a growing northwest wind. At 2:00 a.m. on December 16, her anchor chains let go, and twelve hours later the wind dashed the vessel against the Point Allerton Bar. Thinking it their only chance of survival, four young mates dove overboard and swam fifty yards for shore through the freezing cold water, hoping to head for the local village. At 4:00 p.m., with the storm still raging, the pilot, Thomas Knox, tied a rope around himself and then linked it to the other people aboard. He then dove overboard and swam to the shore with the others in tow. Once ashore, he stood, turned and pulled the rest onto the beach behind him. Together they headed for the safety of the Humane Society hut of refuge, but once inside were disappointed to find just a small bundle of wood, with no means of lighting it.

But relief was on the way. Thanks to the efforts of the young ship's mates, the people of Hull Village were already on their way, ready to start a strong, soul-warming fire inside the hut. Once simply observers during storms, and then wreckers and salvagers in their aftermath, everyday citizens on the South Shore were becoming active lifesavers.

Six months after the wreck of the *Elizabeth*, on June 14, 1803, John Sylvester John Gardiner, assistant minister of the Trinity Church, delivered a sermon at the semiannual meeting of the Humane Society of the Commonwealth of Massachusetts, charting the course for the future of the Humane Society. He orated,

> It may not, Gentlemen, be impertinent to the subject of this discourse, and to the occasion of our present meeting, to remark on a late invention, which appears to be highly useful, in the preservation of human life.
>
> The invention I mean is the Life-boat, the honour of which is due to Mr. Greathead, a boat-builder, at Shields, in England; for which he has received, independent of small gratuities from private societies, one hundred pounds sterling from Trinity House, and a grant of twelve hundred from the British Parliament. This boat contains thirty persons with ease, can neither sink nor overset, and rides, with perfect security, where no other floating machine could exist. The price of a ten-oared boat, which is the largest, amounts to one hundred and sixty pounds sterling.

The minister continued his sermon by describing the boat's design and then made his pitch to the trustees.

> Would it not be advisable, to procure a model of this boat, with an accurate description of its capabilities? If the expense should be found too great for ships to furnish themselves with it, or even for private societies to supply, could not the humanity of the Legislature be excited to raise a tax for this purpose? A few boats of this kind, distributed along the coast, and stationed at places, where shipwreck is most common, might be the means, of saving, in the course of time, thousands of valuable lives to their country and friends.

The society's first action in regards to the construction or purchase of a lifeboat came in 1807. Reverend William Emerson wrote,

> It has been one of the objects of the Humane Society to provide a life boat which may prove the means of preserving many mariners coming upon our coasts in the seasons of storms. There is one now building at Nantucket, which will be finished in a few weeks, and exhibited in the harbour of Boston. It is not yet determined what part of the coasts is best to keep the boat the ensuing season, but generally thought it will be somewhere near the shores of Plymouth.

The first lifeboat ever placed on the shore of the United States for use in potentially saving the lives of mariners in distress at sea found a home in Cohasset. The purchase of the lifeboat and its "shed" was the single most expensive purchase to date for the Humane Society. Cohasset stood out on the Massachusetts coast for its treacherously rocky coastline. Offshore, several sunken ledges, just feet underwater at low tide, lurked with evil intent. Prior to the arrival of the lifeboat, the best a sailor could hope for was to steer well clear of the ledges or, if blown near them by overpowering winds, to have the end come quickly.

Although Nantasket Beach and the mouth of the harbor had proven to be an active shipwreck zone by 1807, and the North River was just ending its heyday as one of the country's great shipbuilding centers, the choice of Cohasset for the placement of the first lifeboat made sense from a practical standpoint. Coming down the coast from the northern end of the South Shore, Boston Light lit the entrance into the approach to Boston Harbor. One Humane Society hut of refuge stood just south of Point Allerton, while another rose out of the sands of Nantasket Beach halfway down the peninsula. The lifeboat guarded the Cohasset coastline, while another hut of refuge guarded the sandy stretch of Humarock below Fourth Cliff in Scituate. Finally, the approach to Plymouth from the north, along the long, sandy stretch of Duxbury Beach, received two

Humane Society crews rode their lifeboats in parades, as recognizable to the locals then as policemen are to parade-goers today. *Courtesy of the Hull Historical Society.*

huts of refuge in 1806. Where sloping, sandy beaches dominated the shoreline, huts of refuge had been deemed satisfactory for lifesaving purposes; where unyielding rock stood ready to claim ships and men, lifeboats would be preferred.

By 1810, the lifeboat had been in place for three years, but had yet to be used for a rescue. News of it, though, covered six pages in the Humane Society's annual report of that year.

> *The life boat belonging to the Massachusetts Humane Society is stationed at Cohasset, under the immediate care and discretion of Captains John Lathrop and Peter Lathrop of that town. She measures thirty feet by ten; in form much resembles a common whale boat, except the bottom, which is much flatter; and is lined with cork inside and outside of the gunwale, about two feet in breadth, and the seats underneath, together with the stem and stern, are filled with cork also.*
>
> *She is rowed by ten men, double backed* [probably should read "double banked"]*, but is fitted for twelve; and steered by two men with oars, one at each end, both ends being alike. Long poles are provided for the men to keep the boat from being drove broad side to the shore either in going off or landing. The poles, about six inches from their lower ends, increase in diameter so as to form a flat surface against the sand, otherwise they would sink into it, and be of no use. Seven hundred weight of the best cork would be sufficient for a boat of her dimensions, but that which was used inside her being indifferent, the weight of her cork is considerably increased. She draws very little water, and, when full, is able to carry twenty people. The boat is also to contend against the most tremendous sea and broken water, and boats of her construction have proved, in England, extremely useful in preserving the lives of shipwrecked mariners.*

Global forces conspired to keep the Cohasset lifeboat from becoming famous for a specific heroic rescue. The year 1807, when the lifeboat made its debut, marked a major turning point in American maritime history. On June 10, the British warship HMS *Leopard* fired into the American warship USS *Chesapeake* off Norfolk, Virginia. The British claimed the ship held Royal Navy deserters, and actually did find one aboard. In the process, though, they had killed three Americans and wounded eighteen others. The American public was outraged.

British impressment of American seamen had been a long-standing problem on the high seas, but the *Chesapeake-Leopard* affair, as it came to be known, took place close to the coast of the United States and incited the American citizenry to call for action from their federal government. President Thomas Jefferson immediately ordered all British ships out of American harbors. In December, Congress passed the Embargo Act of 1807, which, strangely, sought to punish American merchants rather than those ships sailing into American ports under foreign colors. The act forbade American ships from entering foreign ports without the permission of the American president.

The Embargo Act had repercussions that shattered American shipping interests. Unable to leave the docks with their cargoes, ships rotted in American harbors. Shipbuilders, like the men of the North River, found orders for new ships drying up.

Coastwise shipping continued, but without the ability to ship lucrative products overseas, the number of American merchant captains sailing ships on the high seas diminished. Fewer ships in motion meant fewer shipwrecks. The lifeboat at Cohasset continued to sit and wait.

Compounding this mess, relations with France had been at a low point since the Quasi-War of 1798. Napoleonic France was not the same France that had sided with and aided the American colonies in their war of independence just two decades earlier. France and England continued to find ways to upset each other's stability. France disrupted Britain's foreign trade, and England interrupted France's. Until the *Chesapeake-Leopard* affair, the United States traded with both as a neutral observer of the other countries' diplomatic problems.

The Embargo Act of 1807 was just the first of three damaging pieces of legislation aimed at stopping the flow of American goods to Europe. In January 1808, Congress passed a second Embargo Act, this one calling for American whalers and coasting ships—sailing with goods up and down the coast of the United States—to post a bond worth twice the value of ship and cargo as proof that those ships would not sail across the Atlantic and deliver their goods to foreign ports. In March, as crushing economic depression struck New England, Jefferson signed into law a third Embargo Act. This third law prohibited the trading of any goods at all with foreign interests and, among other regulations, stated that port authorities had free will to seize ships and trade goods from captains they suspected had even contemplated smuggling their goods overseas.

Smuggling became the key word of the day, as some American merchants found they had no choice but to return to the days of the American Revolution, when risking running blockades to sell their goods on foreign shores had been deemed a patriotic act. The Embargo Acts were repealed in 1809, only to be replaced with the Non-Intercourse Act, prohibiting trade with France and Great Britain. As a result of these turbulent years, much American capital was moved from the shore to mills and factories.

The acts became just one of the reasons for the commencement of the War of 1812, which lasted well beyond that calendar year. When American embargoes ran out, British blockades, and even attacks on shipping along the coast like the famed burning of ships in Scituate Harbor, kept the industry down.

Affected by these same forces, the Humane Society shifted its focus and its financial resources as well. While they concentrated on building and endowing hospitals, their lone lifeboat at Cohasset continued to sit unused. By 1813, the lifeboat, once a symbol of hope for the cause of humanity, was gone.

In the midst of all the strife, in 1811, a former sailing captain and burgeoning philanthropist named Benjamin Rich began his career as a trustee of the Humane Society, an association that would last for thirty-three years. Rich had lost a younger brother to the sea in 1804, and in 1818 he became a lifesaving hero himself. In May of that year an explosion aboard a Canton packet tied up in Boston Harbor endangered the lives of all aboard. Rich, then forty-two years old, leapt onto the deck through the dancing flames, disregarding the possibility of secondary explosions, and rescued the crew.

In 1829, Rich became the ninth president of the Humane Society, a position he would hold until 1843. During his tenure he had the privilege of launching the society into what historian Mark Anthony DeWolfe Howe describes as its "golden age," from 1840 until the successful restructuring of the federal United States Life-Saving Service in 1871.

Rich's greatest accomplishment came in the wake of the "triple hurricanes" of December 1839. The storms hit the Massachusetts coast with terrific force. "The whole shore of Massachusetts was strewn with wrecks and dead bodies," wrote Sydney Perley in his 1891 *Historic Storms of New England*, "and the harbors of Newburyport, Salem, Marblehead, Boston, Cohasset, Plymouth and Cape Cod were almost literally filled with disabled vessels." An estimated three hundred ships were wrecked, $1 million in property was lost and approximately 150 sailors lost their lives, leaving hundreds of widows and orphans of the sea from Cape Ann to the islands.

Having been a mariner himself and knowing the pain of such loss, Rich inwardly wept for the people of his native Cape Cod, where the storms struck particularly heavily. Acting as president of the Humane Society, in January 1840, Rich joined the trustees in expressing a desire to reenter the world of organized shore-based lifesaving of mariners in distress at sea, but found that the coffers of the society would not yield sufficient funds to construct any new boats.

In April 1840, the state legislature sent a communication to the surprised trustees, a resolve passed on March 21, providing "that there be allowed and paid out of the Treasury of the Commonwealth, to the President and Trustees of the Massachusetts Humane Society, the sum of five thousand dollars, for the purpose of furnishing Life Boats to be stationed at the most exposed parts of the seacoast within this Commonwealth." In a letter dated January 4, 1841, the Humane Society informed the legislature that eleven boats had been constructed and placed appropriately from Plum Island to Martha's Vineyard, including one at Nantasket Beach and one at Cohasset, adding that a boat paid for by the society would be placed at Scituate Beach.

The following year the state approved a $1,350 grant to the Humane Society for the same purpose, allowing them to construct and place more boats. In his report to the legislature in January of 1842, Rich told the story of the success of the lifeboats by alluding to the rescue of twenty-eight lives, but also warned governmental leaders of the importance of maintaining a rigid schedule of boat repair.

> In the gale of the 17th of December last, when the ship Mohawk *was cast on shore at* Nantasket Beach, *when the life boat stationed there was launched into the surf, and, in endeavoring to save the crew, she was driven on the rocks and badly stove. Since which she has been brought to the city and is now repairing, will be finished soon and re-placed in its proper station, the cost of which will be from sixty to eighty dollars. These boats will be constantly wanting repairs, painting &c. &c., and it will be necessary that a small appropriation should be made for that purpose.*

During the mad scramble to save the *Mohawk's* crew, Captain Moses Binney Tower, the keeper of the Humane Society's boats in Hull, did not notice that a fifteen-year-old boy had jumped into the lifeboat, grabbed an oar and started to pull. When he finally did see that young Joshua James had joined the men on the way to the wreck, Tower deemed it too late to turn back. It would be just the first of many lives James would save over the course of his life.

By 1845, eighteen Humane Society lifeboats guarded the Massachusetts coastline; by 1876, America's centennial year, that number had expanded to sixty, including boats in Hull, Cohasset, Scituate, Marshfield, Duxbury and Plymouth. Volunteers from each community proudly served their fellow men, living by a motto spoken by Francis James of Hull: "I'd like to think if I was the one out there, someone would come for me."

The golden age was just beginning.

THE BIRTH OF
THE UNITED STATES
LIFE-SAVING SERVICE

To be part of a "golden age" of lifesaving of mariners in distress, one must live in a time of many shipwrecks, and that's exactly what Americans were doing by living along the coast in the middle of the nineteenth century.

The nation, less than a century old, was still being explored, with new natural resources being discovered that would eventually become trade goods. Westward expansion into Ohio, Tennessee and other territories, made simple by the construction of the Erie Canal and the Cumberland Pike—which also facilitated the return of goods from the newly opened farmlands—increased the quantity of farmed goods being shipped by the United States. American cotton was the king of those crops, made so by the 1793 invention of the cotton gin by Eli Whitney. The invention and proliferation of the railroad increased the rapidity with which goods moved from the interior to the country's major port cities for distribution to foreign purchasers. The growth of the United States depended upon the safe transport of those goods.

By the 1840s, the federal government of the United States had taken several steps toward increasing the safety of seagoing travel and cargo transport. The first lighthouse constructed in the United States, Boston Light, shined forth from Little Brewster Island, north of Hull, in 1716 (earlier aids to navigation intended to guide mariners into Boston Harbor had been constructed in Hull as early as 1673, and probably consisted of nothing more than a lighted bowl of pitch or tar atop a tall pole on either Allerton or Telegraph Hill). Elsewhere on the South Shore, Gurnet Light station was established in 1768; Scituate Light was finished in 1811, just in time for the commencement of the War of 1812; and Long Island Light in Boston Harbor shone forth for the first time in 1819.

A group of civic-minded Boston residents, in an organization mirroring the Humane Society and its efforts, stood behind many of the federal government's navigational safety improvements along the Massachusetts coastline, especially as they affected the movement of ships and goods into and out of the port of Boston. Founded in 1742 as the Fellowship Club, the Boston Marine Society took a royal decree to "make navigation more safe" to heart and set sail on a multicentury journey of improving the lives of

Tragedies along the shore caused outcries for a federal lifesaving system. *Engraving from* Frank Leslie's Illustrated Newspaper, *1878.*

sailors approaching the Massachusetts shore. Since 1791, the Boston Marine Society has appointed pilot commissioners for the port, who in turn have appointed pilots who guide ships into Boston Harbor. The trustees offered advice in the placement of lighthouses, buoys and other navigational aids, helped chart Cape Cod Bay and provided monetary relief for the families of members who died on the sea.

The formation of what would become the Revenue Cutter Service on August 4, 1790—still celebrated today as the birthday of the United States Coast Guard—showed that the United States would vigorously fight for tax revenues due the young country. A debt of $70 million had accrued during the eight years of the Revolutionary War, and, literally, the nation could not afford to let tax revenues slip by. Unfortunately for supporters of the new government, the Revolution had also made heroes of the men and women who had risked their lives to smuggle goods past British customs collectors. Howard V.L. Bloomfield, in *The Compact History of the United States Coast Guard*, wrote that enforcement of the tariff would have to be strict, and undoubtedly would be unpopular, for the "Treasury Department was expected to make good taxpayers of Americans who disliked authority, who had become, through a century of practice, expert at dodging the King's taxes, and who had just fought a war to escape such burdens entirely."

Francis's metallic surfboats, named for the man who made them, inventor Joseph Francis, served as the first lifeboats used by the U.S. Life-Saving Service. *From the collection of William D. Wilkinson.*

Charged with collecting those tax revenues, Secretary of the Treasury Alexander Hamilton built what amounted to the Treasury Department's own navy (in fact, in 1798 during the Quasi War with France, the revenue cutters acted as the American navy), described by Bloomfield as "ten armed revenue cutters, small, swift and manned by stout American sailormen unafraid of man or weather." The fourth revenue cutter, the *Massachusetts*, was launched from Newburyport on July 15, 1791, captained by John Foster Williams, a member of the Boston Marine Society. The sloop served for just fifteen months before being sold, and was replaced the following spring by the *Massachusetts II*. Among the many missions eventually tasked to the "Revenue Marine Bureau" was the 1832 general order to patrol the coast of the United States in winter to aid ships in danger of going ashore, becoming inextricably entangled in ice floes or potentially facing myriad other problems associated with being at sea during the coldest months of the year.

Also in that year of 1832, the federal government began systematically charting the coast, providing mariners a fighting chance against the abundant but hidden shoals and ledges that lurked close to shore in relatively shallow water. And in 1838, the United States began methodically providing inspections for steamboats and their engines.

So, by 1848, America had established trade with many nations (the $70 million debt had been paid off in 1796), constructed more than two hundred lighthouses, marked the major channels with buoys and other aids to navigation, established a seagoing wintertime search and rescue service, formed a steamboat inspection service and begun charting the coast. In Massachusetts, sailors that slipped past all of these safeguards and still wrecked their ships could find their way to safety either under their own power in huts of refuge or could be rescued by volunteer lifesavers heading out in small boats at their own peril. Elsewhere in the United States, though, that final, important piece of the lifesaving network had not been put in place.

The Manby mortar gave inspiration to future line-throwing gun research. *Courtesy of J. Paul Barnett, South Bend Replicas.*

The idea of providing a fleet of vessels for the potential rescue of sailors in peril did not begin with the Humane Society of the Commonwealth of Massachusetts, or even with the Royal Humane Society in Great Britain. Chinese lifeboats had been placed on the Yangtze River in the Middle Ages. According to Clayton D. Evans in "Towards a Humanitarian Ideal" in *Wreck & Rescue Journal*,

> *In Portugal as early as 1691, King D. Pedro II had issued an edict that the Masters of all coastal forts make every effort to render aid to those shipwrecked within their immediate scope of influence. In Great Britain, a permanent charitable trust had been established in 1751, not far from Tynemouth at Bamburgh Castle, its principal goal being the salvation of those shipwrecked in the area. In 1769, an effort was made in The Netherlands to extend humanitarian relief from shore to sea when a series of rescue boats were proposed for the West Frisian Islands. Eventually, the humanitarian ideals espoused by the national lifesaving societies would find common ground with more localized interests, particularly of a commercial nature, and Humane Societies would begin to appear at specific ports or geographic areas. These societies were centered around major trading zones such as Liverpool, Dublin, Oporto, Seville and Boulougne. A great deal of the incentive for creating these organizations came from parties with vested interests in saving ships, cargoes and seafarers (most probably in that order), namely ship-owners and underwriters. In 1802, in fact, Lloyd's of London established the first "life-boat fund" with the aim of establishing lifeboats at strategic locations all along the coasts of the United Kingdom. It would be these local humane societies which would extend*

In a perfect scenario, station keepers in the early days of the Life-Saving Service would have had no problem finding volunteer crews to rush to shipwrecks. *From* Harper's Weekly, *1878.*

the lifesaving concept in Europe and the New World beyond the mere provision of assistance to those fortunate enough to make it ashore, to that of providing waterborne rescue with the use of dedicated lifeboats and crews. The original humane societies and later the lifeboat services would become, in many countries, the first secular charities and their cause would, eventually, appeal to a broad spectrum of national society soliciting donations from both the upper echelons of the populace as well as the common man.

In 1824, Great Britain and the Netherlands created their national lifesaving services, with Portugal, Spain and Prussia following suit. The Belgian Lifesaving Service, the first successful government-funded lifeboat service, founded in 1838, still operates today.

Evans's contention that the creation of lifeboat societies around the world was fostered by desires to save "ships, cargoes and seafarers (most probably in that order)," while sounding callous toward humanity in general, is solid. While human life was important, what governments and owners of mercantile interests truly needed most was that safe delivery of cargo. The Humane Society of the Commonwealth of Massachusetts bucked that trend, forming for exactly the opposite purpose, but for the United States at large, economic needs ruled the day.

Humanity itself was on trial in the years just prior to the Civil War. The unprotected nature of the New Jersey shoreline in particular had garnered attention from that state's government. A horrific February 1846 storm drove nine ships ashore on thirty-five miles of coast on the approach to New York Harbor, and outcries against supposed looting and illegal salvaging reached the ears of the state legislature. "As a consequence," wrote Robert F. Bennett in *Surfboats, Rockets and Carronades,* "an investigatory commission was appointed by the Legislature of the State of New Jersey. The report of that commission, dated March 1846, revealed that of those nine vessels, efforts to assist were made in each case by the inhabitants of the coast. Their aid resulted in the saving of 64 lives of the 110 imperiled."

The days of the "mooncusser," though, were not that far in the past. Although it is trendy today to dismiss the idea that shore-based pirates set false lights on moonless nights (bright full moons revealed more of the nighttime world than did moonless evenings; as such, the looters and murderers who set up the lights would cuss at full moons on cloudless nights), there was once a time when the act was as patriotic as smuggling. During the early days of the American Revolution, British Vice Admiral Samuel Graves sent out a warning in late July 1775 "to All Seafaring People: This is to give notice, that the light house on Thatcher's Island and the light house at the entrance of Boston harbour, are burnt and destroyed by the rebels. And further notice is given, that all seafaring people be careful that they are not deceived by false lights, which the rebels threaten to hang out, in order to decoy vessels into destruction." There is no reason to believe that mooncussers did not exist along the most isolated sections of the Massachusetts coast, or along any other American shore (Nags Head, North Carolina, derives its name from the act of placing a light around the neck of a horse, and thus faking a ship's captain into thinking another vessel lay ahead). Mooncussers were simply highwaymen or train robbers of their day. Ships moving into and out of American ports carried cargoes that could potentially set a man up for life if he brought the right one ashore.

To bring consistency to the potentially rowdy scene of the removal of cargo from a vessel that had come ashore, insurance companies worked with local citizens on building the industry of "wrecking," the orderly and systematic salvaging of any goods still retaining any value after the shipwreck incident. A local "wreckmaster" took control of the situation and kept the underwriters apprised of all that occurred. According to Bennett,

> *Pirates need no definition: clearly they were and are the outlaws of the seas, preying always on those mariners who are helpless before them. In one context, they could travel in armed vessels seizing and looting as they pleased among the unarmed vessels they found. Or they could base themselves on shore and use small craft to board and loot any vessel foolish enough to venture close aboard them, or hapless enough to strand upon a favorite pirate shoal.*
>
> *It is safe to assume that although there were such illegitimate wreckers, the great bulk of the coastal inhabitants of the early United States were ethical persons of good moral character who engaged in wrecking as a legitimate business, if and when the opportunity arose. That they made personal gain out of the misfortunes of others is of little consequence; that those same wreckers saved thousands of dollars of property and many lives, at the risk of their own lives, is significant.*

Prior to the February 1846 disasters, the federal government had made one little-remembered attempt at establishing a lifesaving service on the shores of the United States. A heart-rending tale of loss unfolded on January 2, 1837, when the bark *Mexico* wrecked on a shoal off Hempstead Beach, Long Island, New York. Driven to the ship's exposed deck when the decks below flooded, 124 passengers and crew stood trembling from fear, exhaustion and freezing temperatures as local residents ashore built a bonfire and gathered the courage to help the strangers in danger of dying just offshore. One man, Raynor Rock Smith, hauled out a small boat and called for a volunteer crew. Men responded, and together they rowed to the ship and back, bringing 7 men and 1 boy back alive.

John R. Spears wrote in the *New York Times* in 1904,

> *The landing of the eight men from the wreck…had brought forth a rousing cheer from the people along shore and from those on the wreck as well. It was the only cry of pleasure heard on the wreck. When no one responded to Smith's appeals for a second crew the silent refusal was seen by the eager watchers on the wreck, and the cheers they had given were turned to cries and shrieks of despair. And these wailing cries, with prayers for help, continued into the night until one by one they were hushed in death.*
>
> *When the storm had ceased and the wreck was boarded, the deck was found covered with bodies that glistened in the sunlight because they were coated with ice. Mothers were sitting crouched over their children in a vain effort to ward them from the stinging spray, and the girls lay with their arms around each other. A few over sixty bodies were recovered, and of these sixty-two were buried in the cemetery at Rockville Centre, where a monument, erected to perpetuate their memory can still be seen, with its quaint inscription.*

The revenue cutters patrolling the winter coast since 1832 under general orders eventually received word that they would now do so by law, as Congress made that task permanent for the service (the task at first fell to the navy). The Treasury Department now hired its lighthouse keepers with their ability to potentially save people in the surf in mind. Raynor Rock Smith received an appointment to the keeper's job at Fire Island Light on Long Island. Furthermore, the government sent U.S. Navy Lieutenant William D. Porter, son of Commodore David Porter and brother of Admiral David Dixon Porter, and then tasked with overseeing the lighthouses from New York to Virginia, to Europe to study lighthouses and other lifesaving appliances. He returned speaking in favor of placing lifeboats at lighthouses themselves.

The topic vanished from national discussion for seven years. In 1845, the secretary of the Treasury sent the team of U.S. Navy Lieutenants Thornton A. Jenkins and Richard Bache to Great Britain, France and Belgium to study lighthouses. In August 1846 they submitted their report, which commented extraneously on the presence of a number of lifeboats at Liverpool. They recommended that a similar system be adopted in the United States. Congressman Robert McClelland of Michigan, chairman of the House Committee on Commerce, on February 25, 1847, moved to appropriate $5,000 for the placement of lifesaving equipment at Atlantic Coast lighthouses. On March 4, 1847, Congress passed legislation appropriating the funds "furnishing the lighthouses or other exposed places where vessels are liable to be driven on shore, with boats or other suitable means of assistance." But the appropriation was never acted upon, and the money remained in federal coffers.

The following year a freshman congressman from New Jersey, Dr. William Augustus Newell, asked that the House Committee on Commerce investigate what could be done to improve the chances of sailors surviving shipwrecks on American shores. Garnering no response from his peers, Newell wrote an impassioned speech in anticipation of adding an amendment to an impending lighthouse appropriation bill. While working as a doctor in Manahawkin, Newell had witnessed the devastation of a shipwreck firsthand on August 13, 1839, when the Austrian brig *Terasto* wrecked on a shoal off New Jersey's then-uninhabited Long Beach Island. Thirteen men drowned before his eyes.

On August 3, 1848, Newell delivered his speech, apparently catching the attention of his peers by offering them the staggering statistics that between April 12, 1839, and July 31, 1848, at least 338 vessels had wrecked along the shores of New Jersey and New York—68 full-rigged ships, 88 brigs, 30 barks, 140 schooners and 12 sloops—and that 122 of those ships had wrecked from February 1846 to July 1848 alone. On August 9, his proposed amendment to the bill "for providing surfboats, rockets, carronades, and other necessary apparatus for the better protection of life and property from shipwrecks on the coast of New Jersey, between Sandy Hook and Little Egg Harbor, ten thousand dollars; the same to be expended under the supervision of such officers of the Revenue Marine Corps as may be detached for this duty by the Secretary of the Treasury" was attached. Bennett wrote that Congress, "eagerly anticipating adjournment, seized upon such an opportunity to avoid dissenting argument over such an innocuous piece of legislation" and voted it through unanimously. As such, the United States Life-Saving Service was born a few days later, on August 14, 1848.

Although the argument could be made that there never was an inappropriate time to begin a federal lifesaving system along American shores, the timing of the act of August 14, 1848, proved to be especially providential, and particularly so for the approach to New York Harbor. Human tragedy overseas was about to change the American landscape forever. "The famine in Ireland caused a large migration into the port of New York around 1847–1851," wrote Van Field in *Wrecks and Rescues on Long Island*. "Large numbers of ships loaded with human cargo were arriving. Passenger rates were lower in winter so the poor were more likely to arrive during the worst weather." Approximately one million Irish men, women and children died during the famine, and one million more emigrated, most heading to the United States.

THE ROAD TO THE
SOUTH SHORE

The Humane Society of the Commonwealth of Massachusetts responded quickly to the news that the government had set aside $10,000 for the foundation of a lifesaving system along the New Jersey shore. In fact, on September 25, 1848, a Humane Society committee consisting of Abbott Lawrence and Robert Bennett Forbes wrote a letter to Secretary of the Treasury Robert Walker asking if they could utilize any of the funds appropriated in either the 1847 or 1848 acts. Before he responded, Walker corresponded with the New York Board of Underwriters to ascertain whether they would work with the department's designated Revenue Marine officer to carry out Congress's wishes as outlined in the 1848 act. They responded affirmatively, and Walker then informed the Humane Society that while the $10,000 1848 appropriation was headed for the Jersey shore, they could have the $5,000 from the 1847 appropriation. On October 17, the Humane Society acknowledged that they had received the money. Three more times in the future would the Humane Society receive funds from the federal government: $10,000 in both 1850 and 1855, and $15,000 in 1870.

The secretary of the Treasury appointed Captain Douglas W. Ottinger to work with the New York Board of Underwriters on the development of the first lifesaving stations along the Jersey shore. The underwriters contacted the Humane Society in Boston for help in formulating a plan, and Robert Bennett Forbes sent off a printed pamphlet on the lifeboats and other equipment used by the society's volunteers for saving life. Thus, the society directly aided in the formative years of the Life-Saving Service.

In January 1849, Ottinger wrote to Congressman William Newell about the progress being made in New Jersey. Eight stations had been selected, and lifeboats and rockets had been tested. Each station would be large enough to house survivors and to hold the above-mentioned equipment. In his letter he stated that he and the underwriters had "called to our assistance several of the most intelligent surfmen of the coast" and that they had helped the committee settle on the Francis metallic lifeboat. He also mentioned the possibility of equipping the station with "life cars," but noted that he had not yet received the approval of the board to expend money on them.

Sumner Increase Kimball took over control of the Revenue Marine Bureau in 1871 and became the only general superintendent the Life-Saving Service ever knew. *Courtesy of the United States Coast Guard.*

Kimball's office had its own seal. *From the Charles McClellan collection.*

Already by early 1849 the theory and practice of firing a projectile with an attached line to a ship had been well established. Sergeant John Bell of the British Royal Artillery devised a line-throwing system in 1791 that utilized the power of a small cannon to toss a projectile four hundred yards. A mortar developed by British Royal Navy Captain George Manby favorably used in a rescue in 1809 became the preferred tool of line delivery for "communicating" with an endangered ship. Rockets were first tested for their line-carrying capabilities in 1807.

A fine line existed between the domain of manned lifeboats and the realm of the line-throwing gun. Ships running into danger beyond the breaking surf beckoned lifeboat crews to row to the rescue; ships wrecking in the near-shore area within the breakers robbed lifeboat crews of the ability to safely do their work. At those times, the lifesavers relied on technology to make the journey to the ship for them. A thin line, which came to be known as a "messenger line," thrown to a ship by a mortar, cannon or rocket could be used for several purposes. Once the rope bridge from ship to shore was established, the lifesavers tied a heavier line, or hawser, to it. The shipwrecked sailors pulled on the first line, dragging the hawser onto their ship. Tying it off to a mast, they enabled the establishment of a continuous loop of line through a pair of pulleys, one ashore and one on the ship, that could support a life car, a two-person, enclosed cabin. In a few decades' time this would be replaced by the breeches buoy, a pair of canvas shorts sewn onto a life ring and suspended by four lines to a traveling block. The lifesavers could haul on the "whip" line and send the life car or breeches buoy back and forth between ship and shore. Should complications arise, such as profuse wreckage in the water frustrating attempts to lift the line above the surface to establish the traveling system, the hawser could be used to simply pull the lifesavers directly to the ship in their lifeboat, giving them a steadying influence in the instability of the surf. Manby utilized this latter system in December 1809 at the rescue of the *Nancy* in England.

Lifeboat technology had also evolved since the placement of the Cohasset lifeboat in 1807. The boat selected by Ottinger and the committee for stationing along the Jersey shore was a design seemingly ahead of its time. "The galvanized iron surf boats were adopted on account of their durability and not being likely to need repairs for a long time," Ottinger wrote to Secretary of the Treasury H.H. Meredith on May 21, 1849. "These kinds of Boats are coming into use very fast and I think them peculiarly suited to surf boat Stations as they are not likely to become leaky and therefore always ready for use. The boats which are at the several stations, have a floating power which will sustain fifteen persons when they are full of water."

The equipment and facilities that would become the core of the United States Life-Saving Service system, even if the organizational name did not yet exist, had come together: a station, a boat and a method for delivering a line to a ship. Congress continued to appropriate money, including $10,000 more on each May 29, 1849; September 28 and 30, 1850; and March 3, 1853. The network of lifesaving stations grew particularly on the shores of the approach to New York.

On the South Shore of Massachusetts, where the Humane Society continued its pressing work, word spread of the construction of a new lighthouse on Minot's Ledge off Cohasset and Scituate. Drilling on the ledge for the insertion of nine iron legs began

Sumner Kimball's counterpart in the Life-Saving Service was the surfman. While Kimball worked from a desk in Washington, D.C., to better the life of the seafarer off the American coast, the surfman walked the beach to give immediate assistance. *Courtesy of the United States Coast Guard.*

in the spring of 1847, and the work of constructing the lighthouse continued for more than two years. As the U.S. Engineering Corps finalized the structure in the fall of 1849, tragedy struck on a nearby ledge, one which would soon fall under the warning rays of the lighthouse. On October 7, 1849, the Irish immigrant ship *St. John* struck on Grampus Ledge in a northeast gale, offering up ninety-nine lives to the sea, which claimed them readily. Two months later, on December 13, 1849, Keeper Isaac Dunham lit Minot's Light for the first time. On April 17, 1851, the lighthouse tumbled into the sea, killing the two assistant keepers on duty, Joseph Wilson and Joseph Antoine.

Following the completion of station construction on Long Island, Ottinger found a surplus of funds outstanding from the Congressional appropriations. He then moved to place twenty-six more lifeboats on the East and Gulf Coasts, from Maine to Texas. Five of these lifeboats were destined for Massachusetts, the first on Norman's Head, an island now known as No Man's Land southwest of Martha's Vineyard and halfway between Block Island and Nantucket. The other four, bonded in the spring of 1853, were planned for three Cape Cod hotspots—Chatham Harbor, Monomoy Point, Hyannis and Cohasset—although the Humane Society seems to have altered these plans.

Over the next two decades the marine safety network on the South Shore continued to evolve. The lighthouse station at Gurnet Point had undergone an 1843 transformation with the construction of twin wooden, octagonal towers (in the years before rotating beacons, American lighthouse theory stated that to differentiate between light stations, multiple lights could be used in place of a single light; on Cape Cod, Nauset Beach showed three lights that came to be known as "the Three Sisters"). In 1856, Narrows Light, constructed at the western end of a winding spit coming off Great Brewster

The beach apparatus, or breeches buoy, became the signature lifesaving technique for the Life-Saving Service. Today it is recreated at historic sites in North Carolina and Massachusetts. *Courtesy of the United States Coast Guard.*

Island and marking the entrance to the channel bearing the same name, shined for the first time. In 1860 a new Minot's Lighthouse supplanted the one lost in 1851. With its illumination, Scituate Lighthouse, to the south, was discontinued. That lighthouse, often confused with Boston Lighthouse by mariners unused to the area, causing unnecessary shipwrecks, had gained a reputation among seafarers as the "evil light."

The Civil War caused disruptions of many kinds around the United States. As nations aligned with either the Union or the Confederacy, international trading partners shuffled. Union blockades of Southern ports and severely strained relations between the combatants led to the near cessation of coastwise shipping. The hard work done by Newell, Ottinger and the rest to develop the country's lifesaving network fell to pieces. Without marine traffic, there were fewer shipwrecks. The stations were looted, the boats used for anything but lifesaving.

By 1869, the Humane Society boasted ninety-two stations of all kinds on the Massachusetts coast: seventy-one boats and dories, eleven huts of refuge and ten mortar stations. In Boston Harbor, Deer Island held two surfboats, while the keeper at Boston Lighthouse kept another. Hull's network, overseen by Joseph Cobb, included a mortar station and a lifeboat at Stony Beach (lifeboats were generally larger than surfboats, and less stable in near-shore conditions), another lifeboat at Point Allerton and a surfboat and two huts of refuge on Nantasket Beach. Cohasset's Alfred Whittington, P.C. Kimball and Thomas Hudson took charge of lifeboats at Cohasset Harbor and Pleasant Beach and a surfboat at Symon's Cove.

The metallic surfboat supposed to be placed in Cohasset seems to have been given instead to the volunteers in Scituate, as the Humane Society's records describe "Large

The success of the breeches buoy system owed much to the ingenuity of Lieutenant David Lyle. *Courtesy of the United States Coast Guard.*

Metallic Boats from the Treasury Department—good models and rather heavy" as being in Gloucester, Eastham, Chatham, Nantucket and Scituate Harbor from 1855 forward. Standard lifeboats also served the Scituate coast under H.H. Sylvester on North Scituate Neck, T.C. Bates at Bass Cove (he also had the responsibility of the metallic boat in the harbor) and John Tilden at Fourth Cliff. Other Scituate equipment and facilities included surfboats at Bass Cove and the Glades and a new hut of refuge, erected in 1857, near Fourth Cliff.

Following the rest of the coastline to the south, Otis Baker watched over the hut of refuge at Rexhame, just south of the mouth of the North River, and George Sears had control of the lifeboat at the mouth of the Cut River in Green Harbor. A lone surfboat at Powder Point served Duxbury Beach, while Cromwell W. Holmes maintained surfboat and mortar stations at Plymouth's Manomet Point. The approach to Plymouth gained a second lighthouse in 1871 with the construction of Duxbury Pier Light.

On the national stage, with the fires of war extinguished, the reunited states could focus once more on their problem of loss of life and revenue from shipwreck and, as with other initiatives to the point in the past, tragic consequences served as catalysts for growth.

Congress's initial appropriations came without provision for paid crews, a fact that did not dismay Ottinger in the slightest. In his letter to Congressman Newell on January 16, 1849, Ottinger stated,

> *The general charge of both the houses and the public property is to be given to some responsible person who resides near the station. These persons are mostly agents for some of the insurance companies, and the "boat's crew" who first boards a stranded ship is employed by the underwriters in preference to any other; and if I may judge from the remarks of the various persons whom I have met on the beach, the boats will be readily "manned;" for I am happy to say that I believe that many persons on the "seashore" of your district enter warmly into the feelings by which you were actuated in obtaining an appropriation for so noble a cause.*

But, as Ralph Shanks stated in *The United States Life-Saving Service: Heroes, Rescues and Architecture of the Early Coast Guard*, "Despite praises sung about volunteerism, the results were a disaster." Congress agreed to pay "keepers" of stations no more than $200 per year in 1854, but made no appropriation to do so until 1857. Even so, paying a single person to be on duty with a lifeboat that required the strength of multiple men to effect rescues was a move that did nothing but validate the efforts of that single individual. Should a wreck occur on a barren stretch of coastline, that keeper might have to walk for long distances to find a single human being, let alone an entire crew.

A series of powerful winter storms in 1870–71 that resulted in a distressing number of marine casualties "graphically illustrated the extent of inept personnel, inadequate stations and equipment and the long distances between stations," wrote Dennis Noble in *That Others Might Live: The U.S. Life-Saving Service, 1878–1915*. Congress reacted with an appropriation of $200,000 on April 20, 1871, directing the Treasury to "employ crews of experienced surfmen" to man revamped, upgraded and new stations. Secretary of the Treasury George S. Boutwell tasked newly appointed Director of the Revenue Marine Bureau (created in 1869 to oversee the country's revenue cutters, lifesaving stations, steamboat inspections and marine hospitals) Sumner Increase Kimball with properly expending the funds. "At the time," wrote Frederick Stonehouse in *Wreck Ashore:*

The United States Life-Saving Service on the Great Lakes, "the Revenue Marine as well as the Life-Saving Service was rife with politics and deeply in need of reform. A clean sweep was needed, and Kimball would wield the broom."

Before spending a cent on new construction or paying a new surfman or keeper, Kimball sent Revenue Marine Captain John Faunce on a fact-finding mission to ascertain the status of the stations and boats already in place. Faunce found the stations too far from each other, most in dilapidated condition and many obviously vandalized. At some stations, most of the lifesaving equipment had vanished, while at others "not a portable article was left." Keepers had been appointed as political favors, and not for their leadership or even rowing capabilities. With this report in hand, Kimball centralized control over the country's lifesaving stations; disseminated standard rules and regulations for employees of the service; tore down, restored or built stations anew; examined shipwreck hotspots in an effort to determine future station sites; and established a board that reviewed the latest research and development projects focused on lifesaving equipment that might be useful to the service.

With great momentum, a new wave of lifesaving station construction, the first in sixteen years, struck the coast from Massachusetts to New Jersey, in 1871 and 1872. Kimball ordered the construction of nine stations along the Massachusetts coast in the latter year, all on Cape Cod. It was just a matter of time before the first federally funded lifesaving station appeared on the South Shore.

GURNET POINT, 1874

The Gurnet gained its name from one of the Pilgrims, Edward Winslow, who described the headland as looking like the nose of the fish of the same name. The twenty-seven acres of the Gurnet had been described as early as 1605 by Samuel de Champlain as being covered with a dense forest of pine trees. By 1638, although not physically attached to the community, the Gurnet became a part of Plymouth. Its position at the mouth of Plymouth Harbor would prove to be of major value for military protection in years to come.

The first permanent settlers to the Gurnet arrived in 1720, and by the time of the American Revolution, its military value proved its worth. The HMS *Niger*, a fifth-rate ship of the line, fired on the coastal defenses in 1776 while attempting to enter the harbor. Less than a century later, the Union restrengthened the works, Fort Andrew, in preparation for potential action during the Civil War.

The same advantages seen by military leaders of the eighteenth and mid-nineteenth centuries—sweeping views of the approach to Plymouth Harbor from atop the headland at the mouth—which had also attracted a lighthouse to the site in 1768, brought the Life-Saving Service to the site in the early 1870s. Among Sumner Kimball's order for the construction of twenty-three what would be known as "1874-type" stations in 1873 came the directive to place one on the Gurnet to watch for shipwrecks. On October 14, 1874, George H. Hall, a Marshfield man noted to have twenty years of experience in handling boats in the surf behind him, accepted the position of keeper of the first lifesaving station on the South Shore.

The station's objective was simply stated, if not simply executed. Watching the approach to the harbor partially required maintaining vigilance over the long stretch of Duxbury Beach to the north. To reach the Gurnet by land prior to 1892, travelers had to take a train to Marshfield and then endure nine miles by carriage over the sand. The construction of the Powder Point Bridge that year shortened that trip by three miles.

But the glacially formed beach did not end at the Gurnet. Instead, the sand curled back off it to the west-northwest, rambling toward another headland, Saquish, off which

LIFE SAVING STATION, LUAUNCHING THE LIFE BOAT

The first Life-Saving Service stations built on the South Shore, like this 1874-type station built on the Gurnet, reflected the architectural styles of the period. *Courtesy of Richard Boonisar.*

The Gurnet Point crew in 1891: Chase Stranger, Dan Graffum, Ben Manter, James Thurston, Danna Blackman, Ben Simmons and Captain John F. Holmes, keeper. *Courtesy of Richard Boonisar.*

laid a substantial island, Clark's Island. The lifesavers tasked with manning the station, which then sat with the lighthouse among a few farmhouses, had two patrols, one to the north along Duxbury Beach and one to the west along Saquish Beach. They walked these beats alone for nineteen years. In 1893, they were met on their north patrols for the first time by counterparts from the new Brant Rock station, the only such meeting point between any of the stations on the South Shore. By that time the men of the Gurnet had seen their first building become outdated and also the construction of their new lifesaving station, in 1892.

Also during those years, the Gurnet crew watched as the landscape around their station changed. Vacationers, a section of the populace that never existed prior to the Civil War, discovered the natural allure of the headland, summer sunshine and sea breezes topping the list. Keeper Hall resigned in 1878, making way for the appointment of John F. Holmes on December 23. A little more than a year later, Hall purchased an old farmhouse on the Gurnet and enlarged it, adding a dancing pavilion. Summer visitors hunted and fished, swam and danced. Those folks who could afford to do so purchased land and built cottages of their own. In 1884, Hall swapped farms with the Boardman family of Lexington, who opened the former Hall place as the Gurnet House.

During the quarter century leading up to 1900, the Life-Saving Service matured, and the crew at the Gurnet, more so than at any other South Shore station, lived through the growing pains. Boats were tested and put into use. The equipment of the beach apparatus, utilizing a basic philosophy dating back to the days of George Manby's mortar nearly a century earlier, fell into place with the perfection of the Lyle gun, tested at the Springfield Armory in the western part of the state. Protocols were set for patrols. Shoulder-harnessed punch clocks carried to "keyposts" held surfmen to strict precision on their patrols.

That's not to say that there were not moments of lackadaisical behavior on the part of the surfmen.

Life-Saving Service, Second District, Gurnet Station, Marsh 25, 1894
Hon. S.I. Kimball, General Superintendent U.S. Life-Saving Service, Washington, D.C.

Sir,
I would most respectfully state that night before last at 9–10 p.m. I arrived on Patrolman Clarence Smith's beat and did not find him. I traveled his beat from that time until 11-30 p.m. and did not see him during that time. About 15 minutes later I arrived at the station and met him in station yard. I told him what I had been doing and asked him where he had been. He replied I will tell you the truth, I have been away with a woman, but I should not have done it had it not been a bright moonlight night. I told him there was no excuse for neglect of Patrol duty.
I discharged him according to instructions contained in paragraph 127 of Revised Regulations Life-Saving Service 1884, and yesterday procured another man in his stead. Until quite recently Smith has been a good man, excellent in a boat, always ready, willing

Surfman Walter D. Kezer models lifeboat crew wear of the 1890s, including his cork life jacket. *Courtesy of Richard Boonisar.*

Here, Surfman Kezer shows off his "summer whites." *Courtesy of Richard Boonisar.*

The new Gurnet station, built in 1892, was a "Bibb #2–type," named for the architect, one of three of the design built on the South Shore. Shown here from the rear, the Gurnet station was actually flipped from the original plans, with its boathouse on the opposite end of the building from both the North Scituate and Point Allerton stations. *Left to right*: Keeper Augustus B. Rogers, Ed Tobin, Albert Rhoden, Walter D. Kezer, Lewis Short, Tom Roberts and Oscar Johnson pose for this 1902 photograph. *Courtesy of Richard Boonisar.*

and cheerful about station duties, and until recently I have had implicit confidence in him. In his previous patrol duties he has many times exceeded the requirements, as on his sunrise and sunset patrols, when the weather has been thick, but would frequently lift, he has almost invariably patrolled to the farthest post, saying to me on his return I mean to do as you have advised, if I err on my duties, err on the safe side.

But Mr. Boardman's hired man (an Irishman) with his bad rum and a woman imported from Boston, have led him astray. Mr. Boardman's place here at the Gurnet is left in charge of his hired man during the winter, he alone occupying the premises, and for weeks past Surfman Smith has visited him quite frequently, and sometimes on his returns I have been informed he has ardent spirits enough down to make the fact quite noticeable. On Thursday last, the hired man had a strumpet come down from Boston (called her his first cousin) with 4 quart bottles of whiskey, and the result was the fall of Smith. While he was absent from his patrol beat he was in Boardman's House in bed with the woman.

Life-Saving Service crews drilled five days each week. Mondays and Thursdays were reserved for the beach apparatus drill, Tuesdays for capsizing the lifeboat and righting it again. On Wednesday the crews practiced with signal flags, and on Friday they worked on their artificial resuscitation skills. Here, the Gurnet crew poses as if about to start their breeches buoy drill. *Courtesy of Richard Boonisar.*

If a dishonorable discharge needs to be recorded against Smith, I would most respectfully ask if a notification of the same may be kept from me, until after Smith gets his pay, for if on the day I receive Smith's check I can inform him that I have rec'd no notice of a dishonorable discharge for, I think I can easily induce him to go with me and pay his bills at Plymouth, contracted during the present quarter, Grocer, Clothier and shoe-dealer, for which I feel bound, as I introduced him to them.
Very Respectfully,
Your obedient servant,
John F. Holmes, Keeper

Even with strumpets and Irishmen around, the barrenness of the Gurnet and Duxbury Beach in winter could lead to some strange circumstances. Keeper Holmes, who resigned from his post less than a month later, recorded the following event on September 7, 1898:

Late in the afternoon 2 men with a horse and wagon crossed the Gurnet bound (they said) to Clark's Island to get 2 cows they had bought there and they went in that direction out of sight from the Gurnet. About 8 p.m. the horse with the wagon attached returned to the

All three Bibb #2 stations on the South Shore, including the Gurnet station, here, survive today. *Courtesy of Richard Boonisar.*

Gurnet the bridle being off the horse's head and hanging to his side, but no men were in sight. As the men had to cross from Saquish to Clark's Island by boat, and as there had been a heavy squall of wind and rain about 7.30 p.m. I sent the 8 to 12 p.m. patrol to Saquish by the inside road (the way the horse had come) to discover the whereabouts of the men. The patrolmen discovered nothing. Then I sent the 12 to 4 patrol to Saquish on the inside track but he discovered nothing. At 6 a.m. I hitched up my team and drove to Saquish and found the men just swimming the cows across from the island to Saquish. I took one of the men in my team, the other following behind with the cows and I drove to the Gurnet where the men found their horse and wagon safe and sound. The men stated that they had the Squall after they arrived at the Island, and as they were not much used to boats, they thought they would be safer to stay at the island all night. The horse they had left unhitched at Saquish thinking he could take care of himself, which he did.

Throughout the history of the Life-Saving Service, stories of odd occurrences on nightly patrols kept the "sandpounders" on their toes. One man in Hull was beaten up and robbed. One surfman from the Cahoon's Hollow station on Cape Cod approached his task with great trepidation, being forewarned of a wild bull loose on the beach. Another man in North Carolina stepped on a razorback hog in the darkness; the pig squealed and ran in one direction, while the surfman squealed and ran in another. A surfman from North Scituate found a dead body on patrol, and figuring no one was looking, went through its pockets, claiming its money. The next night, he claimed to feel a slap across his face while standing on the same spot, and threw the coins into the sea. Another surfman walking a Cape Cod patrol heard a gunshot ring out, and was soon engaged in a gun battle on the beach with another surfman over a woman.

Surfman Joseph L. Wixon had none of those problems. Instead, he had to face one of the scariest potential problems of all. On November 6, 1898, new Keeper Augustus Rogers reported on an incident that illustrated just one of the dangers of the beach patrol. At 11:50 p.m., Surfman Nelson King reported to Keeper Rogers that Wixon had never returned from his 8:00 p.m. to midnight patrol, and that his Brant Rock counterpart had arrived at the Gurnet station. Surfmen intending to meet other surfmen on patrol were instructed that if that man never showed up, they should continue walking. "I immediately dressed myself and called all hands," said Rogers, "and with permission to use Holmes' team (after getting a supply of blankets and some whiskey, which was taken from the station supplies) proceeded at once to look for him." Taking the Brant Rock surfman with him in the carriage, Rogers instructed the rest of the surfmen to take kerosene lanterns and walk the inside and outside sections of the barrier beach to look for their fellow lifesaver. Surfman Edward Tobin stayed behind to watch the station. Rogers instructed that if any surfman found Wixon, he was to burn a red Coston signal flare.

Rogers said,

> We at once separated and proceeded up the beach myself with the team going ahead. After we had been about 2 miles met Wixon coming back. I asked him what the trouble was, he stated that when he was walking along the beach within about ¾ of mile of the Post House, the Lantern exploded, and he supposed that he must have fainted, because the first thing remembered he was on the top of the beach looking for the Post House. He had a cut on his left hand in which he carried the lantern.

Rogers took Wixon aboard the carriage, and together they rode back to the station. Wixon showed Rogers where the explosion had torn his lower left pant leg to shreds. The surfman mentioned that the leg hurt as well, but didn't say much more on the ride home.

Rogers dropped Wixon at the station and then headed for Holmes's place to return the borrowed horse and carriage. Before he could finish with the horse, Rogers saw Surfman King run into the yard. Wixon had a deep cut on his leg, and it had obviously bled freely for quite some time. Rogers returned to the station to find Wixon feeling faint from the loss of blood, and began to dress the wound. The lifesavers administered some whiskey, which helped put Wixon to sleep for the night. The next day, Wixon returned to his home.

Eight days later, he returned to duty. His timing could not have been better, as in November of 1898 the lifesavers of the South Shore would need all the help they could get.

MANOMET POINT, 1874

By virtue of one day's delay in the appointment of its keeper, the Manomet Point Life-Saving Station in Plymouth is here listed as the second federally funded station to be opened on the South Shore. Stephen Holmes, age thirty-seven years, accepted the position of keeper on October 15, 1874, twenty-four hours after George Hall took the job at the Gurnet.

Plymouth, tucked away on the western shore of Cape Cod Bay, lays claim to the title "America's Hometown," the site where Elder William Brewster, Captain Myles Standish, Governor William Bradford and the rest of the Pilgrims set up Plimoth Colony in 1620, the first permanent nonindigenous settlement in the New World. And although hidden as it was by the outer arm of Cape Cod, the harbor at Plymouth, protected by the southeast-reaching Duxbury Beach and the northwest-stretching Plymouth Long Beach inside that, became an important and active port over the next century and a half.

The fleet of whalers, coasters, smacks and packets that called Plymouth Harbor home was nearly decimated by the British during the American Revolution. By 1807, the fleet had regained its strength, but President Thomas Jefferson's Embargo Acts forced many of those ships to rest at anchor for months upon end. Only around 1820 did Plymouth's mariners once again begin to profit from their work.

The true growth of the harbor, though, began in 1824 with the opening of the Plymouth Cordage Company. In 1810, America boasted 173 ropewalks. Rope made the maritime world of the early nineteenth century move just as much as did wood or sailcloth. "Nothing symbolic of the sea could be complete without a piece of rope," wrote Frederick William Wallace in *The Romance of Rope* in 1932. "It has bound the world together. It is enshrined in the sailor's heart because the cast-off mooring line is the last link with the land—last to leave and the first to go ashore." The constant flow of raw materials to the Plymouth Cordage Company, when coupled with the goods needed for other local iron and textile factories, made Plymouth Harbor one of the busiest spots in New England by the late nineteenth century. By 1899, Plymouth was supplying one-seventh of all the cordage in the world.

This 1874-type station may be the first Manomet Point station. *Courtesy of Richard Boonisar.*

Sumner Kimball and the Life-Saving Service recognized the importance of the mercantile interests of Plymouth Harbor to the nation soon after the service's 1871 rebirth, beginning construction of both the Gurnet and Manomet Point in 1873, both in the 1874-type architectural style. The Life-Saving Service saw these stations as a stylistic step up from earlier station designs, melding Carpenter Gothic and Stick-style architectural elements. According to architectural historian Wick York in *The United States Life-Saving Service: Heroes, Rescues and Architecture of the Early Coast Guard*, the 1874-type stations "featured an ornate exterior treatment, particularly in the use of scroll work detailing beneath the eaves." Little more than a boat room with a loft above, the first station at Manomet Point served both Holmes and his successor, Miranda R. Sampson, who took over in October 1884, well. In 1901, a majestic "Duluth-type" station, named for the city in which the design was first constructed and featuring a tall, prominent lookout tower, supplanted the old station, which remained in use as an auxiliary boathouse.

Because of its positioning on a high cliff and its proximity to that cliff's edge, the new Manomet Point station had a peculiarity all its own. The boat room doors that would normally be prominent on the front of the building instead were placed on the inland side of the station, to protect the surfmen from tumbling over the cliff with their equipment in the adrenaline-pumping frenzy of the first few moments of a rescue effort.

A decade after the construction of the new station, a significant construction project changed maritime traffic patterns off Plymouth forever. The opening of the Cape Cod Canal on July 29, 1914, meant that ships that had rounded Cape Cod to reach Plymouth and Boston for nearly three centuries could now sail under the protection of the Cape itself and bypass the waters off the Great Beach. For Plymouth, though, the change had come too late. Many of the industries that had made the town strong had failed, although the foresight of the proprietors of the Plymouth Cordage Company who skillfully sought new markets for their products in the wheat and oil fields as American shipping changed from sail to steam kept that particular business alive. Nevertheless, easier access to Plymouth Harbor from the south did not spur an economic upturn for the town. The surfmen and keepers at Manomet Point and the Gurnet, and eventually

The later Manomet Point station, a "Duluth type," featured a prominent cupola for observation of passing ships. *Courtesy of the National Archives and Records Administration.*

the crew of the auxiliary station built at the eastern end of the Cape Cod Canal in 1919, now stood watch over a parade of ships passing by offshore, most of which would never fall prey to the dangers of the harbor's channels. Somewhat symbolically, the first ship to pass through the Cape Cod Canal, the Hull to Boston steamer *Rose Standish*, was captained by Osceola James, the son of famous lifesaver Joshua James of Hull. Six months after the opening of the canal, the Life-Saving Service became part of the new United States Coast Guard.

The 400-foot, 5,284-ton New York to Boston steamer *Robert E. Lee* was headed north after passing through the Cape Cod Canal in near-blizzard conditions on the evening of March 9, 1928. It was a day on which composer George Gershwin sailed for Europe to perform his "Rhapsody in Blue" for that continent's classical music devotees for the first time, and on which George "The Saginaw Kid" Lavigne, the world's second lightweight champion under the Marquess of Queensberry rules, heard the bell ring for the last time, dying at the age of fifty-four. And in a landmark decision, a U.S. Circuit Court judge ruled that Native Americans should not be held accountable to U.S. naturalization laws and should be allowed to cross the American-Canadian border at will, as recognized by the Jay Treaty of 1796. These news stories would be lost on the people of Plymouth, pushed to the back pages of the newspapers by an unexpected and unnecessary local tragedy.

As the *Robert E. Lee* pressed northward that night, snow, sleet and hail entering the wheelhouse driven by forty-five-mile-per-hour winds hindered Captain Harland W. Robinson's ability to navigate his ship. The thick atmosphere shrouded the twin fourth-order Fresnel lighthouse lenses seven miles to the north at the Gurnet, aids intended to help mariners steer clear of the hazardous Mary Ann Rocks. Without their help, Robinson was in trouble.

The *Robert E. Lee* missed the first set of rocks, but struck and ran hard aground on the second. The vessel began to ship water on its starboard side, and Robinson ordered the seacocks opened, settling the *Lee*, and then sent out an immediate SOS distress call. At

The cupola and the cliff on which the building sat gave the Manomet Point station crew a commanding view. *Courtesy of the National Archives and Records Administration.*

midnight, with high tide just two hours away, he feared for the safety of his passengers and crew. But the stranding had been so relatively gentle that some of the 273 passengers slept through the entire incident.

Ashore, Boatswain's Mate William Cashman and the Coast Guard crew at Manomet Point attempted to contact the stranded steamer by flashing light for over an hour. But the fog that had settled in rose and fell in such a pattern that it made communication impossible.

Feeling unsure of the situation, Cashman called his men to the station's pulling surfboat. After several attempts at launching their boat in the pounding surf in the darkness, they opted to wait for sunrise. After the turn of the tide, the *Lee* stabilized, and some of the passengers took to singing songs to pass the time. When the sun rose, one man awoke and headed for the onboard barber's shop for a shave, unaware of what had transpired during the night.

At first light, Cashman and his crew—Frank Griswold, Edward Stark, Alden Proctor, Irving Wood, Joseph Ducharme and a local mechanic named Ernest Douglas who volunteered to go out in place of Arthur Young, who was sick at home in Orleans—launched the surfboat onto the still-churning seas and headed for the *Lee.*

The 125-foot Coast Guard patrol boat *Bonham* had arrived on scene during the night, as had the Coast Guard destroyer *Paulding* and the 178-foot cutter *Tuscarora.* The 125-foot patrol boat *Active* and the 75-foot patrol boat *CG-176* stood by as well. Cashman climbed aboard the *Lee* and talked with the ship's captain about the alternatives for removing the passengers and crew to safety. Both agreed that rowing them to shore in the surfboat would be a long, tedious process, and that shuttling the passengers to larger vessels would be their best course of action. The Coast Guard had also dispatched two 36-foot motor lifeboats during the night, one from Wood End station in Provincetown at the end of the Cape Cod peninsula and one from the auxiliary station at the Cape Cod Canal, to the scene. Once the first transfer had been made, just after 11:00 a.m., Cashman and his crew headed for shore, confident that the situation had been correctly tended to. By the end of the day, every person on the ship would be safe on dry land.

The *Robert E. Lee* stranded on Mary Ann Rocks on March 9, 1928, within the area of responsibility of the crew of the Manomet Point station. *Courtesy of the Old Colony Club of Plymouth.*

As the Manomet Point crew approached the shoreline, though, tragedy struck. A wave, described by one of the Coast Guardsmen as twenty-five feet in height, lifted the stern of the craft, jamming the bow into the seafloor, pitch poling it on top of the crew. The seven stunned men floated helplessly in the water, shocked and injured by the boat's unexpected overturning. Two hundred spectators watched onshore as Surfman Griswold momentarily surfaced and then sank out of sight. Boatswain's Mate Cashman clung to an oar as Surfman Stark complained to his friends Proctor, Ducharme and Wood that he had a severe pain around his heart. Wood, who believed that the gunwale had struck Proctor when the boat flipped, helped push him onto the overturned vessel.

Local residents Russell Anderson, Earl Harper and Massachusetts state trooper John Horgan scrambled to the shoreline, where they found a leaky dory. Cutting it loose, they rowed toward the drowning men. From around the point lobsterman Harry F. Eddy and friend Daniel Sullivan rowed another dory to the scene. Anderson and crew pulled Cashman, Proctor and Wood into their boat while Eddy and Sullivan grabbed Stark and Ducharme to safety. Civilian Douglas told them, "I can hang on. Take someone else first." Griswold could not be located.

The Wood End thirty-six-foot motor lifeboat arrived on the scene and transferred Proctor, Douglas, Wood and Stark to the *Paulding*, which headed for the Chelsea Naval Hospital in Boston Harbor. Ducharme and Sampson were taken to Plymouth's Jordan Hospital. Twenty-seven-year-old Edward Stark died in transit.

On the beach, Dr. Edgar Hill and Fire Chief Albert E. Hiller worked on the unconscious form of Boatswain's Mate William Cashman for a little more than two hours before pronouncing him dead. A priest on the scene performed the last rites. Surfman Frank Griswold's body washed ashore a day later.

In the days that followed the tragedy, as ten thousand sightseers packed the roads leading to Manomet Point, the people of Plymouth looked for answers to seemingly simple questions. Why had the federal government allowed the men charged with protecting the coast to work in a building with no toilets, heated by coal stoves and lit

On the morning of March 10, 1928, the Coast Guard crew from Manomet Point launched their lifeboat to aid the *Robert E. Lee*. Three men in this picture died on the return journey. *Courtesy of the Old Colony Club of Plymouth.*

only by kerosene lamps? Why should there not be a lighthouse erected on Manomet Point to more effectively steer ships away from the Mary Ann Rocks? And why, nearly three decades after the introduction of the service's first motor lifeboats, were these men manually rowing to the scene of a rescue? In the end, the locals surmised, the Coast Guardsmen of Manomet Point had been left powerless to save their own lives.

Two months after the disaster, the people of Plymouth gathered outside the Manomet Point Coast Guard Station to dedicate a simple memorial to the fallen Coast Guardsmen. Dedicated on May 30, 1928, to the memories of Boatswain's Mate William E. Cashman, Surfman Frank W. Griswold and Surfman Edward P. Stark, the plaque on the stone reads, in part, "Greater love hath no man that this, that a man lays down his life for his friends." The same Biblical passage was carved onto the grave marker of Joshua James, and serves as an all-too-familiar reminder of the deadly risks taken by America's lifesavers when mariners are in distress at sea.

FOURTH CLIFF, 1879

The Fourth Cliff Life-Saving Station knew only two keepers during the Life-Saving Service era: John Smith and Fred Stanley. John Smith took the position on September 3, 1879, and left the service on September 22, 1880. That day, Frederick Stanley, who had joined the service as a surfman on January 18, took over as the head of the station. He held the position for thirty-five years, until March 22, 1915, retiring at the age of seventy. Along the way, he saw a lot of shipwrecks and he saved a lot of lives.

Scituate's first three numbered cliffs were all thickly populated well before what is probably the most famous cliff of all: Fourth. When one examines the topography of the town of Scituate, it's easy to see why. Scituate's natural harbor sits north of First Cliff. First and Second Cliffs shield the landward approach to them across Edward Foster Road and the marshland it traverses. Third Cliff offers the same convenience with access via the Driftway. But Fourth Cliff has always stood alone.

The fact was that when Scituate was settled, a beach connected Third and Fourth Cliffs, albeit in a tenuous way, and the rest of the land now known as Humarock was a southward-reaching peninsula. It made no sense for Marshfield to claim it, for there was no landward approach to it from their town, with the North and South Rivers flowing out from between the southern end of the peninsula and Rexhame. The irony today, of course, is that for Scituate residents to get to Humarock by land they have no choice but to go through Marshfield. So, with no access from the Marshfield side, and limited access from the Scituate side, Fourth Cliff became a tough sell for farmers looking to till the Scituate soil.

One family, though, the Tildens, were up to the task, as generations lived on the cliff over the course of centuries. Nathaniel Tilden, who arrived on the *Anne* in 1623, built his house on Kent Street and soon became one of the wealthiest men around. "He had left a comfortable, not to say pretentious home in England for a rude dwelling here," said Harvey Hunter Pratt in *The Early Planters of Scituate*, "that he might obtain the greater spiritual solace of an unhampered devotional." Among his holdings were extensive parcels of salt marsh inside "New Harbour," the basin inside Fourth Cliff.

The Fourth Cliff station opened in 1879, as the Life-Saving Service began moving northward along the South Shore. *Courtesy of Richard Boonisar.*

The last Tilden homestead on Fourth Cliff was built in 1828, but the family would not be alone for much longer. The Humane Society of the Commonwealth of Massachusetts erected huts of refuge at Fourth Cliff in 1787 and again in 1857, leaving the latter in the care of John Tilden, who also had control of the society's lifeboat there as late as 1869.

Around this time, too, came an early boardinghouse. As described by Joseph Merritt in *Anecdotes of North River and South Shore*, looking from the Driftway toward the cliff "a lone two story building and an old barn were for a long time the only structures to be seen. This was the Fourth Cliff House, one of the first summer boarding houses on the South Shore. Long before the days when summer people were coming in any number to Scituate and Marshfield a few families who had discovered the place and liked the quiet were in the habit of spending their vacations there." William Merritt and family arrived to run the Fourth Cliff House in 1879, catering heavily to shorebird hunters each spring and fall. That same year, the Life-Saving Service built its Fourth Cliff station at the southern end of the hill (it was known as "Scituate" until 1883, when the service changed its name to "Fourth Cliff").

Born on January 27, 1845, in Boston, Fred Stanley lived the life of a typical lad of his era, educated in the city schools until the age of twelve and then sailing off to sea as a cabin boy. The *Biographical Review for Plymouth County, 1897*, recorded,

> *He followed the sea until he was twenty-three years of age, circumnavigating the globe more than once, doubling Cape Horn and the Cape of Good Hope, and visiting the principal maritime countries of the globe. The harbors of London, Liverpool, Havre,*

The *Chattanooga* wrecked off Hewitt's Point in Marshfield in 1888, making for a long trek for the Fourth Cliff crew. Its wreck and that of the *Agnes R. Bacon* that same year may have led to the opening of the Brant Rock station in 1893. *Courtesy of Historical Research Associates.*

Cronstadt, Calcutta, Australia, New Zealand and the Brazilian ports became almost as familiar to him as old Massachusetts Bay, and before he was twenty-five years old he was an all-round citizen of the world.

Retiring from the sea, he took up fishing and Irish mossing in Scituate before joining the Life-Saving Service.

Irish mossing, an industry almost entirely confined to the coast of Scituate during the latter half of the nineteenth century, made good boatmen out of many of the town's young men. Rowing out two hours before low tide in flared fourteen-foot boats, Irish mossers reached over their gunwales with sixteen-foot rakes to drag *chondrus crispus*, a red algae, from the rocks below. Dried, Irish moss yielded carrageen, used as an emulsifier in many products, including beer in the mid-1800s. The industry drove Scituate's economy off and on for decades. A summer harvest, Irish moss allowed its gatherers to consider other work during the colder months. The schedule dovetailed perfectly with the lifesaving business, which, for everyone at the station besides the keeper, took June and July off.

During his life at the station, Stanley assisted approximately forty large vessels. Occasionally, the major rescues came in bunches. At 5:30 a.m. on February 11, 1888, a patrolman from the Fourth Cliff station saw a light well to the south of the end of his patrol through a blinding snowstorm. Unable to discern whether the light emanated from a ship, he returned to the station and informed Keeper Stanley. Stanley headed south, and as the snow cleared, without doubt he saw a schooner upon the beach at Hewitt's Point, four miles to the south of the station. Knowing the crew would never get their lifeboat to the scene through the ice floes moving offshore, he ordered it hauled by land south to the mouth of the North River at Rexhame. Getting into the boat, the lifesavers crossed to the Marshfield side and continued their trek southward, reaching the scene at 11:00 a.m. The local Humane Society crew had attempted a rescue, but failed when ice overwhelmed their oars and tholepins.

The ship's hull had been submerged by the frigid water and the crew had scampered into the rigging. With the beach frozen solid, the lifesavers could not dig a hole in which to place their sand anchor, a heavy wooden cross with a ring to which the shore end of the breeches buoy hawser would be attached, a crucial step in erecting the system. Instead, they buried it under the heaviest rocks they could find, hoping that would hold the anchor. Stanley aimed and fired the Lyle gun, needing only one shot to deliver the line into the grasp of the crew as their vessel began to break up. Each man stepped into the breeches, and one by one the lifesavers pulled them ashore. According to the 1888 *Annual Report of the Life-Saving Service*, "On no trip did the occupant of the buoy touch the water." The sand anchor held. Stanley later learned the name of the vessel, the *Agnes R. Bacon*, of Morristown, New Jersey, moving from New York to Boston with a load of coal.

Just four months later, the bark *Chattanooga* of New Haven stranded on nearly the same point of land. As the wreck occurred in late June, at a time when America's surfmen were off making a living on their own for two months, Keeper Stanley had to rustle up a crew. He found two of his regular surfmen and convinced five volunteers to join them in racing to the scene in the station's surfboat. Telegraphing for a tugboat to meet them at the scene, the crew rushed to the wreck. About forty-five minutes after they arrived, the ship sank with its cargo of salt from Puerto Rico. Stanley and his makeshift crew brought the crew of nine and their single passenger ashore in the surfboat, transporting them and their luggage to the local train station, even using his influence to arrange for them free passage to the city. After returning the surfboat to the station, Stanley and his two surfmen headed back to the wrecked ship to protect it from potential illegal salvaging, staying aboard for two full days until the captain returned.

Five months later, in late November, Stanley witnessed what may have been the oddest incident in his entire lifesaving career. The dismasted Boston fishing schooner *Edward H. Norton*, drifting helplessly off Scituate with sixteen men aboard during a terrific late fall snowstorm, capsized, sweeping fourteen of the sixteen men to their deaths in the icy depths. Two men miraculously stayed with the ship as it wandered upside down toward the shore, striking on First Cliff.

Surfman William H. Murphy spotted the wreck at 2:00 a.m. and found a body in the surf. Burning a Coston flare to determine whether others had survived the ordeal, he found nothing and returned to the station with the news. Keeper Stanley opted to wait until the south patrol returned to be sure no other ship needed immediate assistance. With no news coming in, Stanley took surfmen Marcus Barber and Joseph Flynn and headed for the wreck of the *Norton*.

"We searched the beaches all along but could find no bodies," Stanley later wrote in his log. "About 8.30 two boys saw a stranger leaning over a wall who told them he came out of the wreck and there was another man in her. At the time could see no way to get under her so I got two axes and cut a hole through the bottom but could find no one." After the tide ebbed, the lifesavers did find someone, the captain, Frank Curran of Boston, entangled in trawl nets in the aft section of the boat. They took the body to the Scituate receiving tomb. The next day, four more bodies washed ashore. In late January, three more identifiable as members of the crew floated in on the tide. In March, two more arrived.

The *Helena*, wrecked in 1909, added one more notch to the belt of Keeper Frederick Stanley of the Fourth Cliff station. *Courtesy of Richard Boonisar.*

The list of vessels tended to by Stanley and his men grew through the years: the schooner *Bessie C. Beach*, drifting aimlessly from the North Shore after losing her rudder, tested the lifesaving crew's piloting skills as they steered it close to the entrance to Scituate Harbor where a tug could pick it up; the schooner *Minnie Rowan* in February 1894 required three launch attempts in a lifeboat to finally save eight crewmen, including a captain with a broken leg; and the schooner *Puritan* in December 1896 called for the rescue of six men by breeches buoy. On November 16, 1900, a man named John Monroe became stuck in the mudflats of the Herring River. Keeper Stanley launched a dory and rowed to his assistance. Offering an outstretched oar, Stanley pulled the man from hip-deep mud. On April 9, 1901, Stanley and his crew rescued five men from the schooner *George S. Boutwell*, named for the secretary of the Treasury who had appointed Sumner Kimball to the position of director of the Revenue Marine Bureau in 1871.

The station itself lived in danger. The Life-Saving Service moved it on its lot in 1893, as the "sea was making dangerous inroads" upon the land.

In 1905, Stanley quietly celebrated his silver anniversary of service to the United States Life-Saving Service. Nine days later he turned sixty years old. Time would begin to catch up with him. Later that year, George H. Brown, keeper at the North Scituate station, his former protégé and later fellow keeper, left the service against his will, due to disability. But Stanley still had one major rescue effort in him.

On November 7, 1908, Surfman Number One Matthew Hoar left the Fourth Cliff station with a leg injury, unsure of when he would return. The following day, Keeper Fred Stanley returned to duty, himself having been out with an infirmity. He had some catching up to do. The crew had received a new Race Point surfboat in October, complete with masts and sails, and they needed to all be proficient in its use.

By late January, Matthew Hoar had still not returned. On January 29, 1909, Stanley lost another of his longtime trusted surfmen, his number two, for an indeterminable amount of time. "At 8.15 a man came to the station with news that the mother of surfman W.H. Murphy had died, so I allowed him to go home," Stanley wrote in his journal.

The following morning, at 6:30 a.m., Surfman Number Six John Carson reported that a schooner, the *Helena*, had come ashore just to the north, under Fourth Cliff, breaking up the crew's breakfast. He also reported that he'd burned three Coston flares in attempts to draw a response from the stricken ship. Stanley, who had turned sixty-four years old three days earlier, examined the vessel's position in the jagged rocks and determined that a breeches buoy rescue would be the best possible way to save the crew. "It was a wicked morning," he told the press. "We could just see the outlines of the schooner and could hear the breakers pounding on the shore all around her." The crew took the breeches buoy up the hill abreast the wreck and fired two shots with the station's Lyle gun. Both found their target, even in the darkness of the predawn hour, but the crew aboard the ship could not see them. As the light developed, the ship's crew found the second shot between the fore- and mainmasts and hauled away. The breeches buoy was rigged and, according to Stanley, they "soon had the 8 men of the crew ashore without any accident. Then cut the hawser and got all the gear back to the station at 11 a.m."

The *Helena* incident did not end there. The following day, the captain of the *Helena* fell out of his ship's rigging. "Surfmen [Dennis] Quinn and [Frank J.] Carlton with an outsider (James Ward) jumped in a dory and tried to get him but owing to the sea running around the bow were unable as every sea would sweep them back on the beach." Imploring the captain to let loose his grip on a rope to which he was holding, the surfmen left the safety of their dory and grabbed him as the sea swept him around the bow of the schooner. Stanley arrived on scene and ordered the man carried to the station, as he could not walk. Surfmen Marcus Barber and John Carson with six bystanders lifted him and transported him to the building. Following standard procedures, the keeper oversaw the removal of his wet clothes, his rubbing down, wrapping in warm blankets and intake of hot drinks. The lifesavers "put him to bed with bottles of hot water round him and he soon fell asleep. In three hours he was all right again."

For the next week, the *Helena* and its scattered cargo of lumber consumed the daily lives of the keeper and crew. On February 8, 1909, "At 3 p.m. a man was brought into the station suffering with a bad wound on his foot, while trying to save lumber from the surf a fellow workman drove an icepick through his foot. We washed it clean and dressed it for him and he was carried home." Due to the abundance of lumber ashore, the crew could not practice the beach apparatus drill on the beach until March 11.

Fred Stanley served his country as a Life-Saving Service keeper until there was a Life-Saving Service no more. When the service merged with the Revenue Cutter Service in 1915, he took advantage of something most of the surfmen and keepers never had access to: a pension. He retired in March 1915 as one of the most prolific lifesavers in the history of the service.

NORTH SCITUATE, 1886

By the time the North Scituate Life-Saving Station opened in 1886, the Life-Saving Service had established itself as one of the foremost organizations of its kind in the world. The level of organization and efficiency that the Life-Saving Service brought to the community, when coupled with nearly a century's worth of local expertise in coastal lifesaving, made the service's arrival on the rocky northern coastline of the town practically seamless.

The Life-Saving Service built the first of its three South Shore "Bibb #2" type stations (named for the architect who designed it, Albert Bibb) in North Scituate. The station, according to architectural historian Wick York, looked like "a cottage residence," essentially and sensibly blending into its surroundings on the beach. Scituate, accessible by train and steamboat, had become a summer getaway spot for Bostonians of the Victorian era, some of whom built seasonal homes on small lots in the Minot area. The lifesaving station stood out for only two reasons: a cupola and a set of large doors that led into the boat room. Knowing that the Atlantic sometimes encroached on the row of houses between the ocean and Musquashcut Pond, directly to the west (during the Minot's Light Gale in 1851 the sea opened a forty-foot section of the beach, halting buggy traffic between North Scituate and Egypt on the beach for some time), the Life-Saving Service gave the station a twist. Normally, the aforementioned boat room doors would face the ocean directly, for rapid deployment of boats to the sea. The sea's reputation, though, caused a ninety-degree turn for the face of the building, with the boat room doors facing the south.

Being the second lifesaving station in town had its privileges, as well. During times of local expansion, the Life-Saving Service usually had no farther to look for its next keeper than the closest number one surfman. In the case of North Scituate, the Fourth Cliff number one, George H. Brown, made the selection process easy.

Born in Boston on July 15, 1841, Brown could trace his Scituate ancestry back at least two generations, with both his father and grandfather being born there. After finishing school in Boston, Brown, the son of a shipbuilder, headed to sea aboard the clipper ship

The North Scituate station, of standard Bibb #2 design, featured a perpendicular turn to the beach. *Courtesy of Richard Boonisar.*

Staghorn at fourteen years old, stopping at many sites in the Pacific. At seventeen, he took up the trade of ship caulker, learning from his father back in Boston until he turned twenty-one.

On September 1, 1862, hearing President Abraham Lincoln's call for 300,000 Massachusetts men to take up arms against the rebel South, Brown enlisted with the Forty-second Regiment Massachusetts Volunteer Infantry for nine months' duty. He was one of eight George H. Browns who fought for Massachusetts during the Civil War. His experiences during that conflict amounted to nothing more than building redoubts and picketing railroads along the Mississippi River near New Orleans, Louisiana. On August 20, 1863, Brown found himself at Camp Meigs in Readville, Massachusetts, to accept his pay and to be mustered out of service.

For two years after his return, Brown ran the schooner *Frank*, built by his father's firm, Brown & Lovell, as a packet between Boston and Scituate, where he met and married

Keeper George Brown, shown here with the tools of his trade, ran a tight ship for two decades at the North Scituate station. *Courtesy of Richard Boonisar.*

Lydia B. Burrows on August 21, 1865. He later ran the sloop *Lady of the Lake* as a fishing boat in spring and fall, taking advantage of her as a party boat in the summer, carrying visitors to Scituate's shore out on pleasure excursions. After selling that vessel, he joined John H. Smith of Scituate aboard the *Bell*, a coastal transport schooner.

On December 7, 1879, the Life-Saving Service appointed the thirty-eight-year-old Brown as surfman number one at the newly built Fourth Cliff station. For the next seven years he learned the trade of lifesaver under Keeper Frederick T. Stanley. On December 15, 1886, he accepted a transfer to the new North Scituate station as keeper, upon the completion of its construction. Between the opening of the station and the keeper's retirement due to disability in 1905, the North Scituate crews responded to three dozen calls of distress, the most memorable of which was the wreck of the brig *T. Remick* on March 5, 1889. The day would be defined by fresh northeast winds, constant rain and continually heavy surf, a typical late winter out-like-a-lion New England storm. But Surfman Thomas Maddock found work for the crew to do well before the sun rose and the day could truly get started.

At 2:20 a.m., Maddock, on the north patrol, saw a bright light shining away to the south. Thinking the station might be on fire, he ran toward the light "as fast as he could

The North Scituate crew, like their brethren up and down the coast, practiced their skills relentlessly throughout the year, as shown here on a Tuesday morning boat drill. *Courtesy of Richard Boonisar.*

until he got almost there when he saw that it was a vessel ashore," according to the station's daily journal. Signaling the ship, letting anybody aboard know that they had been seen, Maddock retreated to the station. He informed Keeper Brown that the ship was about three hundred yards away. Leaving the station with their surfboat, the crew arrived at approximately 3:25 a.m. and prepared to launch into the crashing surf.

But there was not enough natural light for the crew to tell exactly where the surf was, and where the distressed ship lay in conjunction with it. They strained their eyes and glinted into the darkness until suddenly a "high sea" barreled into them, filling their boat with water. They took the boat to higher ground and bailed it out. They soon realized that the ship, which they recognized as a brig, was now so close to shore that a straight surfboat rescue would be tricky at best, and deadly at worst. Brown improvised.

Braving a few steps out into the surf, the lifesavers tossed a heaving line—a line with a weight at the end to facilitate a distant toss—onto the deck of the ship. The men aboard made the line fast and watched as the lifesavers retreated to shore for their boat. Taking a page from George Manby, of mortar fame, they aligned their boat with the line and used it to pull themselves to the wreck. Ten men waited on the deck. The lifesavers retrieved all ten and brought them to the station safe and sound, as the wreck disintegrated behind them. The ship and cargo were a total loss, but the entire crew survived.

Beach apparatus drills often attracted crowds, and the lifesavers often allowed bystanders to participate in the breeches buoy drill as "victims." *Courtesy of Richard Boonisar.*

Brown and his men were featured in a *Boston Globe* article in 1892, an embedded reporter–style tale of a day in the life of a Life-Saving Service station. One of the stars of the article, and of the *T. Remick* rescue, Surfman Thomas Maddock, had a small but interesting impact on the history of the Life-Saving Service.

Born to a commission in the Royal Navy in Waterford County, Ireland, Thomas's father John Thomas Maddock ran away from home at age twelve after a heated argument with his father. Immediately signing onto an English ship as a cabin boy, he set out for the sea. When that vessel tied up in Boston, he signed onto another for a two-year voyage, and soon found that the sea would be where he felt most comfortable, and where he would spend the bulk of his life.

Before the outbreak of the Civil War, John met and married Katherine Murdock, a native of Bristol, England, just across the water from his native home in Ireland. Relocating from Boston to North Scituate, they built a home and started a family. Together they had two sons, Thomas and Alonzo, and two daughters, Jennie and Laura.

Born August 8, 1859, some of Thomas John Maddock's earliest memories concerned his father returning home from his many months away at sea. "The children looked forward to their father's return from his long voyages," stated author Vincent L. Wood in *Plum Island Recollections*. "He always had little souvenirs from foreign ports hidden away in his ditty bag. When the time was near for his arrival, Laura would shinny up the flag pole where she could see her father turn down the lane toward the house. When he appeared she would slide to the ground and race up the lane to be the first to greet him." Before his children were fully grown, John tired of the long, lonely days and nights on the open ocean, and traded in his ditty bag for a Boston Harbor pilot's license. "The children all remembered the messenger in the middle of the night tossing pebbles against the window pane and calling "John Maddox—John Maddox—a ship is in!' His children remember the messenger pronouncing his name as though it ended with an 'x,'" wrote Wood.

At twenty-four years old, on January 10, 1884, Thomas married eighteen-year-old Florence Mabel Cushman of Scituate. Two months later, on March 26, their first son, Richie Snow, was born. Two years later, on April 7, 1886, Willard Cushman Maddock, a second son, entered the world.

Faced with a growing family and the need to obtain a steady, reliable paycheck, Thomas left the life of a carpenter behind and signed up to be a surfman at the North Scituate Life-Saving Station on March 1, 1887, where he would learn the trade under newly appointed Keeper Brown.

Described by Margaret Cole Bonney in *Scituate's Sands of Time* as being "5 feet 4 inches tall" and "of dark complexion with black hair" and blue eyes, Maddock put his "knack of putting things together…shown in many fine pieces of workmanship around the station" to good use for the benefit of his lifesaving brethren, or at least he tried to do so. By 1894, already a veteran of seven years of patrolling the beaches of Scituate, Maddock presented two inventions to the United States Life-Saving Service's Board of Life-Saving Appliances that he felt would help to lighten the surfmen's load.

The board's official report on Maddock's patrolman's signal case described it as being

> *made of stout leather…4½ inches long, 1½ inches wide, and 3½ inches deep. It is fitted with straps for suspension from the shoulder or the waist of the wearer. The interior is divided into compartments for holding two signals, and there is a place for the signal holder or firing appliance. A device of similar material for the same purpose, although much larger and heavier, was adapted some time ago, but gradually fell into disuse, because the leather, when wet, damaged the signals rather than protected them. The Board is of the opinion that the tin cases now used give general satisfaction and that the introduction of the Maddock case seems to be unnecessary.*

Undaunted by the board's rejection of his first proposed labor-saving device, Maddock tried again in 1899 with a belt and holder for Coston signal flares.

Not every moment was hectic. Although not originally a military job, Life-Saving Service duty entailed a lot of "hurry up and wait." *Courtesy of Richard Boonisar.*

This belt is intended to be worn on the outside of the clothing. It carries a Coston signal holder and two copper Coston-light cases. While this device shows ingenuity in construction and simplicity in operation, the experience of the board has been that if worn on the outside of the clothing there would be a liability, in stormy and freezing weather, of the holder becoming so clogged with ice or frozen snow that it would be impossible to use it without first thawing it out. The separate copper case, for the protection of the signal lights when carried in the pocket, is of the same size and construction as the tin cases now in use, and does not possess any great advantage over them. The Board is of the opinion that it would not be advised to recommend the adoption of either of these articles.

Although he found himself again turned away by the Board of Life-Saving Appliances, Maddock by 1897 had impressed at least one important official, superintendent of the Second Life-Saving District, Benjamin C. Sparrow, who made him one of the first beneficiaries of the service's adoption of civil service rules the previous year.

From its very beginning, the USLSS held a practice of hiring lifeboat captains and crews from the populations nearest the stations, to allay fears that would otherwise arise concerning visible federal government presence in small coastal communities. That system, though, eventually faltered, as keepers' appointments became political favors, and many imperiled seamen soon found their lives to be in the hands of untested, unskilled and in some cases downright-afraid-to-launch-a-boat lifesavers. In 1896, after reconsidering the service's hiring and promotion practices, General Superintendent Sumner Increase Kimball announced the immediate implementation of civil service standards. Promotion from surfman to keeper would henceforth be determined by merit, and would be made on a district-wide basis.

Thomas and Florence Maddock had brought five more children into the world since he had joined the USLSS. Catherine Florence, born February 27, 1888, sadly died of whooping cough less than three weeks later, but Jay Thomas (May 19, 1889), Ralph (July 12, 1891), Ruth (July 24, 1893) and John Alden (July 11, 1895) were all healthy and growing in 1897. With all of those mouths to feed, Maddock could hardly afford to turn opportunity and Superintendent Sparrow away when they came knocking. With ten years of lifesaving experience along the Scituate shores behind him, Maddock accepted the post as keeper of the Merrimac River Life-Saving Service station in Newburyport, Massachusetts.

Maddock spent twenty-two years in control of the Merrimac River station, becoming one of the most well-known citizens of that area, retiring in 1919. Heeding the advice of his father concerning family relations ("Guard your temper well, for mine has cost me dearly!"), he turned the station into a social center, training his sons and nephews to man the building during the summer breaks, and leading singalongs on the banjo and cello, always sharing the company of two or three St. Bernard dogs, the patrolmen's best friends. After his retirement he built Bonnyview cottage, furnished with rugs made from his beloved St. Bernards and a distinctly discernible entryway, marked by an archway formed of two whale ribs still attached to their vertebra, known as "Captain Maddock's Wishbone." There he spent his remaining years with his second wife, Alice Hawthorne.

Thomas John Maddock died on July 4, 1945, and was buried in full-dress uniform in West Concord, New Hampshire, the hometown of his wife Alice. Were it not for the introduction of the civil service rules into the Life-Saving Service, Maddock may well have eventually taken over the North Scituate or Fourth Cliff station. Instead, he traded South Shore for North Shore, a Scituate native who succeeded in life, but left his mark outside of the town's borders.

POINT ALLERTON, 1889

After nearly half a century of lifesaving along the shores of the town of Hull, the volunteer lifeboat crews of the Humane Society of the Commonwealth of Massachusetts were about to be joined by the federal government in their battle with the unscrupulous fury of wind and wave of New England winter storms. The earliest Hull lifeboat crews, under Captain Moses Binney Tower, launched into the breakers in search of shipwreck survivors in 1840. In October of 1888, one of Tower's crewmen, Joshua James, then in his sixties, was still at it, taking up the sweep oar as the keeper of the Humane Society's boats in Hull.

According to the *Hingham Journal* of October 26, 1888, the United States Life-Saving Service had finally decided to take up position at the mouth of Boston Harbor to supplement, or even replace, the volunteer crews. "Proposals were opened last week in Washington," read the *Journal*, "for the construction of the Point Allerton, Hull life-saving station, and which will be in commission before the end of next summer." The brief article went on to describe the building, which was of standard design used elsewhere in the country. "The rooms are all spacious and well ventilated, and every provision has been made for the health and comfort of the men." It was, in fact, an exact copy of the station built in North Scituate just two years earlier.

The *Hingham Journal* of November 23, 1888 (the day after Joshua James's sixty-second birthday), reported the big news that "Superintendent Kimball of the Life-Saving Service has made the award for the construction of the life-saving station, at Point Allerton, Hull…The station will be fully equipped and in running order by next winter." The timing of the announcement could not have been more coincidental. Two days after the newspaper hit the streets, a storm for the ages hit the South Shore.

Joshua James and the volunteer lifesavers representing the Humane Society, some of the same men who would soon be wearing the uniform of the United States Life-Saving Service, worked for the next day and a half to save lives along the Hull coast. They responded to five wrecks, including a three-masted schooner named *Gertrude Abbott*. The *Gertrude Abbott*, with 825 tons of coal and headed from Philadelphia to Boston, had

Joshua James and his Point Allerton crew oversaw the approach to Boston Harbor. *Courtesy of the Hull Historical Society.*

With multiple medals from the Humane Society and the federal government, the venerable keeper Joshua James was the most decorated lifesaver in the history of the United States. *Courtesy of the United States Coast Guard.*

struck the Toddy Rocks hard, seemingly beyond the reach of the Hunt line-throwing gun. The captain, John Thompson, ordered the American ensign flown upside down, a recognized call for help from ashore. James and his men moved their equipment up the beach to the scene and dug a pit for the placement of the sand anchor, but the captain ultimately concluded the rescue would need to be effected by use of the lifeboat.

With the tide approaching its highest point, and darkness falling across the scene, James directed his men to build a large bonfire atop Souther's Hill, a bluff overlooking the disaster scene. The lifesavers planned to wait for the tide to ebb, but due to the fury of the storm, no noticeable change occurred in the power of the surf. The captain discussed the dangers of the impending rescue with his men. "Captain James warned his crew that the chances were they would never return from the attempt to save the shipwrecked men," wrote Sumner Kimball in his 1909 biography of James, "but asked who were willing to go with him and make the effort." James later stated that he felt "the danger of the crew of the vessel was also fully understood if a rescue was not attempted on the next low tide." His men faced a grave choice, to risk their own lives now so others might live, or wait out the storm and know that the shipwrecked sailors would probably die. Some of the volunteers turned their life jackets over to others from the crowd who were willing to face the odds, and the lifeboat filled with would-be lifesavers.

The trip seaward, taken between 8:00 and 9:00 p.m., was as dangerous as James imagined it would be. Having grown up on the beaches and waters of Hull, he knew every sunken stone, every protruding rock like a brother. "The boat was repeatedly filled," wrote Kimball, "as the huge waves swept over it, disputing every inch of the way and often forcing it back into imminent peril of being dashed to pieces on the rocks." Two men were detailed to do nothing but bail water out of the boat, as the seas, "running mountain high," continuously assaulted the *R.B. Forbes* and its crew as they battled their way through the breakers.

After a strenuous pull, the lifeboat arrived alongside the *Gertrude Abbott*. The lifesavers tossed a heaving line aboard the schooner, which the ship's crew made fast on deck. One by one, the sailors tied the ropes about their waists and timed their leaps with the crests of the waves, diving with fragile faith into the outstretched arms of the tired, wet and cold lifesavers below. Eight times over this pageant played out, each man finding temporary safety from the storm in the arms of his fellow men, until the entire crew had made the jump.

Now, though, with the lifeboat *R.B. Forbes* weighted down with twice as much humanity as on its trip to the wreck, the lifesavers turned to the task of returning to shore and navigating the Toddy Rocks with the surging waves pushing them from behind. Hindered by the presence of the eight survivors, the lifesavers worked the oars as best they could, but the storm soon took the upper hand. About six hundred feet from shore, the boat struck a rock and rolled to one side. Oars flew away and one of the lifesavers was tossed from the boat. The crew shifted their combined weight to windward and righted the craft, simultaneously pulling their displaced fellow lifesaver back aboard. "I called to the men as loudly as I could to stick to the boat," related James, "no matter what might happen."

Shipwrecks like the *H.C. Higginson*, wrecked in the Great Storm of 1888, kept the lifesavers of Hull busy. *Courtesy of Richard Boonisar.*

Those words, of course, were easier understood than adhered to under the current circumstances. The boat crashed toward the shore, alternately hitting rocks and being swung through green water at the whim of the sea, all the while the lifesavers using what few oars were left to push the *R.B. Forbes* free of obstructions and on a general course toward the beach. "It seemed like a miracle that she was not thrown bottom up by some of the breakers when striking the rocks," said James.

Finally, though, such a situation unfolded. The boat struck a rock that opened a gaping hole in the starboard side, but the lifesavers and those whose lives they saved realized they were in shoal water, and close enough to the shore to scramble to safety. Mrs. Esther Reed beckoned the survivors to her home, where they found warmth, food and comfortable beds for the evening. The lifesavers continued to work, rescuing a total of twenty-nine men during the Great Storm of 1888.

Eleven months later, on October 25, 1889, Joshua James walked into the new Point Allerton Life-Saving Station and took note of the supplies that arrived at the station: "Received this day 25 envelopes Supt., 27 Form 1809, Journal Form 1808, Letter Paper 2½ quivers, 24 Official Business envelopes, 10 Blotters." And with those innocuous words, the Life-Saving Service era began in the town of Hull.

At midnight on Saturday, March 1, 1890, James's crew arrived for duty. Eben Tower Pope and Joseph T. Galiano, both married to daughters of the keeper, donned the numbers one and two. George F. Pope and John W. James, his nephews, took the numbers three and four, while his great-nephew, Francis Bernard Mitchell, wore the number five. Louis F. Galiano, the brother of Joseph, wore number six, and William Hunt, the only man not related to Joshua James on the crew, wore the number seven surfman's uniform. The regulations of the service forbade nepotism, but then, they also stated that no one over forty-five years of age could be hired as a keeper or surfman, and Joshua was by then sixty-three years old. A public outcry on his behalf forced Sumner Kimball to allow the hiring.

Joshua James and his lifeboat crews pulled off some of the most dramatic rescues in Life-Saving Service history. *Courtesy of the Hull Historical Society.*

As for the nepotism, well, there was little James could do about that. Hull in 1890 was a town of 450 permanent residents. The most experienced and storm-tested surfmen in town—Mitchells, Jameses, Popes, Cleverlys and Galianos—came from essentially the same bloodlines. John Boyle O'Reilly, a summer resident and champion of James and his work (on the second day James was in the new station, O'Reilly sent over copies of six of his books for the crew to have on hand), asked that Kimball allow the appointments, "for," he said, "all our regular Hull fishermen are intermarried in the most extraordinary way."

Unfortunately, even those years of experience could not prevent accidents from happening. James reported on Monday, March 31, 1890, just a month after opening the station, "While practicing today, about 3 p.m. Surfman No. 5 Louis F. Galiano while getting into the Breeches Buoy from Drill pole, the traveling block ran on to his hand, causing him to let go. He tried to grasp the Breeches Buoy, but missed it, and grasped the small whip line, which ran through his hand, burning it some, he fell to the ground, about 15 ft striking on his feet. At first appeared not much hurt, but later was taken sick to the stomach, vomiting with severe distress in the stomach. Took him in the Station, put him in bed, applying hot cloth, soaking his feet in mustard water, which relieved him. The resident physician being absent, telegraphed for Dr. Spaulding, Hingham, who arrived in an hour. He examined him but apprehended nothing serious, a severe jar, ordered him to lie in bed two days on his back. Will call again Wednesday."

With Galiano out of service, James pulled an ace out of his sleeve. Although Kimball had allowed James's appointment, he denied one other that the keeper had hoped for,

When Joshua James died, his crew transported him to his final resting place the only way he would have wanted to go—by lifeboat. *Courtesy of the United States Coast Guard.*

that of Alonzo Lovell Mitchell as his number one surfman. But they had broken the rules once, appointing a sixty-two-year-old. At forty-six, Alonzo Mitchell was a year too old. As soon as a spot opened up for a "T.S.," or temporary surfman, Mitchell got the call.

The work of Joshua James and his Point Allerton crew would become legendary. Remarkable rescues made under the most appalling of meteorological conditions for the next decade solidified James's status as the greatest lifesaver the United States had ever known. In some incidents, as with the *Ulrica* rescue in 1896, the entire crews received recognition. At other times, the extent of James's work went almost unnoticed.

At about 11:00 p.m. on Friday, July 3, 1891, one of the local steamboats, the *General Lincoln*, "ran over a small boat off Long Island, and sunk her," James said in his report the next day. A man and three boys who were on the boat struggled in the water as the steamer's crew threw life preservers overboard and lowered their lifeboat, "succeeding in taking them all from the water in about 12 or 15 minutes. The boys being able to swim got hold of life ring and were all right, one boy holding on his father, although he was under water 8 or 9 minutes and was insensible when taken from water."

The pilot of the steamboat immediately began performing artificial resuscitation on the man, the exact method used by the Life-Saving Service on their Friday drills. That was no coincidence; the man who ran over the small boat was Joseph Galiano, Joshua's son-in-law, and his former number two surfman. "The jaws were not clinched [*sic*], at first, but some minutes after became so, having to be forced open with piece of wood inserted. It was 50 minutes or more before there were any signs of life."

In the meantime the steamer pulled into the Pemberton landing and the keeper was called to help restore the dying man. Being the off-season, James was alone at the station.

"On arriving, found him breathing with difficulty, and suffering...pains in lungs and back—applied mustard plasters, hot flannels to stomach and armpits, hot water bottles to limbs and feet. He continued to suffer and about 3 a.m. called doctor who gave hypodermic injection soon after he went to sleep." The man awoke before 6:00 a.m., still feeling very weak. James dug through the chest of clothing donated to the station by the Women's National Relief Association and found some that fit. Galiano took the man back to Boston, "fully restored, but very weak."

In time, the Hull lifesavers found that although Mother Nature threw her best at them, they had seen it all before. They responded to wrecks on Toddy Rocks, Point Allerton and Nantasket Beach. They rescued crews with the breeches buoy and by lifeboat, and used unorthodox methods as well. They improvised where necessary, but never lost their cool.

At 12:30 p.m. on February 8, 1899, with a thick snowstorm blowing out of the east, Surfman Fernando Bearse discovered a vessel pushing in toward the shore about two miles southeast of the station, precariously close to stranding on Nantasket Beach. Gauging the power of the wind and snow, James sought aid from his neighbors, asking Miss Floretta Vining for the use of two horses to pull the beach apparatus cart to the scene, and imploring James Dowd, a former surfman and the owner of Knight's Express livery service, to lend the crew two more to pull the Humane Society's lifeboat to the impending wreck. The crew reached the spot at 2:00 p.m.

"On arriving found the vessel was not ashore," wrote James, "but was riding at anchor just outside of the outer breaker, in a very dangerous position. As there was a very heavy sea and as she was liable to come ashore any minute, the LSS crew, made their headquarters at the half way house intending to stay all night." The halfway house, a shelter built at the turnaround spot for the south patrol just that year, was "large enough to accommodate the LSS crew and a vessel crew," according to James. When the sun went down, the lifesavers returned one pair of horses, stabling the other nearby. At 11:30 p.m., five members of the crew returned to the station, with the others planning to spend the night in the halfway house. "At midnight the wind changed to NW and the vessel swung offshore, comparatively safe," wrote James. With the clearing wind, the crew could now read the name on the vessel: the *Gertrude Abbott*.

While Joshua James may not have seen everything before that night, he certainly had seen this.

BRANT ROCK, 1893

The transformation of Brant Rock took place in the blink of a historical eye. Marshfield's earliest settlers set up their farms and fishing stations in the southern end of the town. Green Harbor is named for one of those first settlers, William Green. The pastoral scene was given an aristocratic air by the arrival of the Winslow family, survivors of the *Mayflower* expedition of 1620 and the subsequent first harsh winter at the Plymouth settlement, and a deeply patriotic tone by the arrival of gentleman farmer and future presidential candidate Daniel Webster in 1832.

Marshfield historian Lysander Richards enticed Brant Rock resident T.B. Blackman to write down his memories for inclusion in the historian's 1901 *History of Marshfield, Mass.*

I have known Brant Rock for sixty years. In those days there was not much to attract people to these shores but the sea fowl in the fall of the year, which then were very abundant. My father visited Brant Rock even before I knew the place; I could not have been more than six years of age. He came down gunning, his gun burst in his hands, and his lower arm was blown to pieces, which laid him up for a long time. It was a great treat in my boyhood days to come to the shore and get lobsters from under the rocks with a gaff hook. I gathered strawberries from the pastures, which in those days were plenty.

I do not remember any house in early days at Brant Rock proper, westerly of the Rock. There was a house located up the beach north from what is now called Ocean Bluff; this was known as the Charity House, in which was kept a stove, a little wood and a few matches. It was provided and equipped by the Massachusetts Humane Society for the mariner when driven upon the beach by storms.

In those days the grass growing on this beach was a source of litigation, many thinking they had a right to let their cattle feed upon it, while others thought this grass a strong protection to the beaches and should not be fed. It hazarded all that property westerly of the beach, and finally an ordnance or law was passed, prohibiting the feeding of the grasses, and in my opinion it was a wise provision and should have continued for all time. These uplands, together with the beach at Brant Rock, were in the early days known as

Keeper Benjamin Manter and his Brant Rock crew pose in front of their boat room doors. *Courtesy of Richard Boonisar.*

Spectacle Island, the upper island forming one eye, the lower island the other. The strip of beach at Brant Rock at this date was but a cartway leading from Marshfield neck through the beach and across the two islands to the easterly side of Green Harbor.

The house in which I now live was built in the year 1835; there was a house on the upper island at this time, but when built is not known; this house was burned in 1835 or 1836. Three houses have burned on that island. When I came here, in 1856, there was but a cartway, with four gates to open to reach my place. There had been some little improvement made in the way at the north end, the slough had been filled with stone, and a bridge was constructed, but across the beach it was mud and sand. I have crossed this beach when I could not go more than the length of my team at a pull.

In 1845 there was a house built at Brant Rock by Samuel Turner of Hanover, Mr. Tribou of Hanson, and a Mr. Jordan; this was known as a gun house, owned by these men. There was a house also at the north end of what is now known as Ocean Bluff by Africa Keene of South Abington. Below and westerly of my house, near Green Harbor river, four small houses were built in 1848 on land of Gideon Harlow. These houses were occupied in the summer by lobster fishermen...In 1853 another house was built

Manter's crew looked equally as resplendent in the summer whites. *Courtesy of Richard Boonisar.*

by Anselm Robinson of Bridgewater, who at that time took a lease of the land and later purchased the same of the heirs of Gideon Harlow.

In 1861, the first year of the Civil war, the Pioneer Cottage was built by Capt. George Churchill, Charles Brown, Edwin Reed, and others, of Boston. They took a lease of the land for five years, but bought it before their lease expired. In 1866 the Churchill Hotel was built and run by George Churchill. Then followed the building of the Wrightman Cottage, the Pierce (south from the hotel), also the Howland & Jones and the George Hatch cottages, the last two being north from the Pioneer. They were built by Samuel Turner. Mr. Walter Peterson built in 1870 or 1871.

The Brant Rock House was built in 1874 and was run by Henry T. Welch of Cambridgeport. S.B. Richmond of Lynn built in 1874. Ocean House, by Paine & Bonney, was built around 1875. Gilman Stetson of South Hanover built the same year. Fair-View House was built by Martin Swift of Bridgewater about 1877. There were many houses built in 1875 and 1876. I have mentioned but few of them.

A lumber yard was established in the fall of 1870 by T.B. Blackman. The lumber was brought from Maine and the West. This made good business till the shoaling of the river, caused by building the dike. Sales of lumber in 1875 amounted to more than $5000, and would have become a fine business but for the shoaling of the harbor and the river.

Left: Brant Rock surfmen patrolling to the south exchanged tags or "checks" with surfmen from the Gurnet station. *Courtesy of Richard Boonisar.*

Below: Breeches buoy drills at Brant Rock, as elsewhere, brought out the crowds. *Courtesy of Historical Research Associates.*

Mr. Edwin Reed built in the year 1881. Charles Sprague built in 1876, and George Thomas in 1878. The highway from the First Congregational church in Marshfield to the Beach was laid out in 1692. From Waterman's Causeway to the land of Thomas Liversidge, a road was built in 1862. From this point through Brant Rock village to the Pioneer Cottage the road was laid out in 1867. The Dike road was built in 1879. From the Pioneer Cottage over Ocean avenue to a point near the house of T.B. Blackman, a road was laid out in 1890.

Without delving into the minutiae of specific house locations, one can see from Blackman's personal narrative that Brant Rock went from a place characterized by remote gunning stands, lobstering, strawberry picking and a lonely "charity house" to one known for its hotels and summertime high life in the span of a generation. A major vehicle for this transformation, literally, was the railroad. The Duxbury and Cohasset Railroad arrived in Marshfield in 1871. "The influx of visitors arriving by horse-drawn barge from the railroad depot at Marshfield increased the need for seashore accommodations at Brant Rock and Ocean Bluff," wrote Cynthia Krusell and Betty Magoun Bates in *Marshfield: A Town of Villages*.

The average American felt the changes of the Industrial Revolution in unambiguous ways. Freedom from the farm and the setting of strict hours in factories and at other jobs in the major cities meant the creation of idle time, once the domain of the devil's work. Those men and women who owned factories or held management positions could now afford to spend free time—sometimes a week, sometimes a month, sometimes an entire season—on vacation.

Vacationing in the late nineteenth century usually meant escaping the sights, sounds and smells of the cities, and replacing them with billowed sails under puffy offshore clouds, open-air band concerts and clambakes. For Bostonians, those luxuries existed just to the south, in Quincy, Hingham, Hull, Scituate and Marshfield, among other towns. Trains, when their lines finally reached those communities, and steamboats could carry families to the seashore with heart-racing speed, at least when compared to the ancient stagecoach. Businessmen who needed to keep their fingers on the pulse of Boston could do so by taking the train to the city in the morning and returning at the end of the workday, before the sun set, still able to enjoy the summer with the family at the shore. Brant Rock—named for the small goose that was once hunted along the shore—went from drab desolation to teeming with seasonal youthful vivaciousness right before T.B. Blackman's eyes.

And into this world, the Brant Rock Life-Saving Station appeared in 1893. The questions "why there?" and "why then?" may well be asked. As for the timing, the placement of the station came several decades too late. The North River shipbuilding industry, as we have seen in the story of the Fourth Cliff station, had died in 1870. And while the mouth of the North River at that time still sat just to the north of Brant Rock in Rexhame, the small flow of packet ships that could actually make their way up and down the shallow river hardly warranted a second station guarding the waterway's entrance so closely.

To the south, the Gurnet station has successfully guarded Duxbury Beach for nearly two decades, and between them, Gurnet and Fourth Cliff had taken good care of the Green Harbor, Brant Rock and Ocean Bluff shorelines. But as the area stretched between the Green Harbor River and the South River, making Brant Rock nearly an island unto itself, the placement of a station there would save the lifesavers at the existing stations the trouble of crossing those rivers should a ship come ashore in the area. From time to time, they did. Keeper Stanley and the Fourth Cliff lifesavers rescued the crews of the *Agnes R. Bacon* and *Chattanooga* on Hewitt's Point in separate incidents in 1888. But

The interior of the Brant Rock station boat room featured, among other equipment, a life car. *Courtesy of Richard Boonisar.*

Launching the lifeboat on Tuesday mornings meant one thing: capsize drills. *Courtesy of Richard Boonisar.*

any new lifesaving station in Brant Rock built in 1893 would most likely be dealing more with summertime revelers with more cash than navigational know-how who would be out on the water in boats of which they had no right to be taking the helm than ships hauling major cargoes during the waning days of the age of sail. And therein may lie the answers to the questions of "why there?" and "why then?"

Sumner Kimball knew the value of public relations. From his earliest days in the directorship of the Revenue Marine Bureau, and his 1878 appointment as the general superintendent of the United States Life-Saving Service, Kimball set out to convey in the best possible use of the English language, without embellishment or exaggeration, the amazing tales of wreck and rescue occurring on America's coastlines. The *Annual Reports of the United States Life-Saving Service* read like adventure novels, with surfmen and keepers dashing out into stormy nights, fighting wind and wave, offering their vitality and even their lives in return for the safety of strangers passing their shores. It was some of the best writing the United States government ever produced.

Yet the annual reports were only one cog in the Life-Saving Service public relations machine. While Kimball purged political favoritism from the service at large, he still understood that political pull offered its advantages. A senator or representative calling for the construction of the station at a certain point along the coast had the wherewithal to make that happen by sponsoring a bill in Congress for the appropriation of money toward that end. The growth of the service depended on the constant goodwill of politicians, and on making sure those politicians were constantly reminded of the service's good work.

As such, Kimball knew that placing a station in a highly populated area, specifically one that catered to moneyed families from the city that had the ears of politicians—a place, say, like Brant Rock in 1893—increased the chances that those appropriations would keep on coming. Certainly, with its easterly facing shore lining the pathway from Plymouth to Boston and the rocky outcropping that gave it its name, Brant Rock could perceivably be a shipwreck magnet. But what Sumner Kimball was sure of was the fact that it would be a high-profile spot that would help spread the word about the good deeds of the Life-Saving Service.

Lifesaving crews often made outreaches to their communities by allowing locals to participate in their beach apparatus drill. Each station was required to perform the drill twice a week, and the monotony of the routine could be dreadful for the surfmen involved. Fresh faces, often of children, and sometimes even those of young women, could considerably brighten the days of the drills. And a show of precision in front of the summer visitors, especially of government money well spent, could go a long way as well.

Krusell and Bates quote from a paper written by Jeannette Hixon Avery about the Brant Rock station's drills circa 1910:

> *Once a month the lifesavers practiced their rescue tactics. The large boat was rolled out and rowed a short distance into the water. On land the small cannon boomed and shot a rope out to the boat. The breeches buoy was the heavy breeches of canvas attached to*

Keeper Benjamin Manter, left, started out as a surfman at the Gurnet station. *Courtesy of Richard Boonisar.*

a ring which was suspended from a pulley running along the rope. This was pulled out, the seaman climbed into the contraption and was pulled to safety. The lifesaver or coast guardsman walked up the beach in the late afternoon until he met the next patrolman from the next station.

And few stations could boast rescues such as this one, which occurred on August 20, 1898, according to the Brant Rock daily journal:

About 4 p.m. a young man who was employed on a merry go round, which is located about fifty yds from the station, while attempting to get on the machine slipped and fell striking a tent pole breaking his right leg above the knee. He was seen by the surfmen and at once taken to the station.

Dr. N.K. Noyes of Duxbury, Mass was at once called accompanied by Dr. Walter J. Graves who assisted in attending to the man's injury. The surfmen rendering all the assistance required. The young man remained at the station until morning when by direction of Dr. N.K. Noyes he was taken to Brockton Hospital. Mr. John Burgess the owner of the merry go round went with him to the hospital.

Yet, whatever the initial reason for building the station may have been, the people of Brant Rock were certainly glad it was there when the storm of the century struck the South Shore in November 1898.

THE PORTLAND GALE
OF 1898

I f Joshua James took time to reminisce when he arose on the morning of Saturday, November 26, 1898, he would have realized that that day marked the tenth anniversary of his finest moment, the Great Storm of 1888, in which he and the volunteer Massachusetts Humane Society lifesavers of Hull, Massachusetts, rescued twenty-nine men from six vessels within the span of about thirty-six hours. The crews that day committed the surfboat *Nantasket* to its first test, and the boat performed admirably enough to silence the experts who said it would never succeed as a lifesaving craft. The dramatic events of November 25–26, 1888, made Joshua James and the surfboat *Nantasket* the most famous lifesaving tandem in the world.

Now, ten years later, Joshua James, who had just turned seventy-two years old four days earlier on November 22, proudly wore the mantle of keeper at the Point Allerton U.S. Life-Saving Service Station in Hull. The *Nantasket* rested quietly halfway down the beach in the Massachusetts Humane Society station number twenty. This station was the headquarters for Hull's volunteer crews, watched over by its keeper, thirty-three-year-old Osceola James, Joshua's only surviving son.

The outbreak of the Spanish-American War led to extra duty for the keepers of the South Shore lifesaving stations and four of the surfmen at each post during the summer of 1898, as they received orders to remain on duty for the summer months and watch the horizon for enemy warships. Until late November, that extra assignment defined the year for each of the crews. Singular incidents up and down the shore kept the crews mildly busy, but as winter approached, it seemed that the season would be a relatively forgiving one.

The first frost arrived in early November. At the Gurnet, Surfman Joseph Wixon, injured when his lantern had blown up in his hands while he was on patrol earlier in the fall, returned to work on November 15. Three days later, on November 18, the keepers of the South Shore lifesaving stations noted an increase in the intensity of the surf. At the Gurnet, Keeper Augustus B. Rogers checked off "strong" for surf in the daily report at midnight and at sunrise, and upgraded it to rough for the rest of the day. Up and

A half-dozen men in a small boat stood no chance against the power of a storm that could do this to the hotels along Nantasket Beach. *Courtesy of the Hull Historical Society.*

down the coast, the keepers kept a close eye on the sea for the next six days, sometimes sending extra men out to patrol during the daytime hours. Only the old veteran from North Scituate, George Brown, downplayed the week's meteorological disturbances; where others checked rough, he checked light; where they marked strong, he said he saw smooth seas.

On the morning of November 26, Brown noted that the sea was smooth from midnight forward. In fact, the disruptive winds and scattered rains from the previous week had dissipated to leave the South Shore with a seasonably chilly, cloudy, breezy but not windy day. Keeper Benjamin Manter took advantage of the lull to run a resuscitation drill with his crew. Afterward, Surfman Nathaniel Besse left to tend to a family illness, replaced by Arthur Manter for the day. By late afternoon, though, the winds returned, shifting around from the west to the east and northeast, howling a bit stronger than they had all week, as dark clouds began to gather overhead.

As the storm approached Scituate and Marshfield that afternoon, Fourth Cliff Life-Saving Station Surfman Richard Wherity felt it was his duty to warn the hunters that annually found their gunning huts on the salt marshes of the North River each November, when migrating ducks made their return to the area, of the impending turn of the weather. But the temptation to linger in the marshes was strong for the hunters. Of particular interest to local sportsmen at that time of the year were the three species of scoter ducks—black, surf and white-winged—which they colloquially called "coots," not to be confused with the American coot, a different bird entirely.

Some gunners looking for coots rowed out along the beach before sunrise in small dories and anchored themselves in long lines perpendicular to the shore. The birds flew in predictable aerial pathways from the north, parallel to the coast, and could be drawn in with decoys. When flights passed overhead in loose formations consisting of all three types of scoters and possibly a few common eiders and oldsquaws (recently renamed as "long-tailed ducks"), numerous guns popped at once and gunners began arguing over who got what before the birds even hit the water. A good day's hunting could net fifteen to twenty birds.

Some gunners, like the Clapp brothers of Scituate's Greenbush section, and the five young Norwell men in the Henderson party on November 26, preferred to do their reconnoitering from small wooden shanties they'd located in the salt marshes. One of the Clapps, Everett, even had his own trained flock of Canada geese to use as live decoys to bring the birds in close enough to shoot.

Once back to the center of town with their catches, gunners had the option of keeping their prizes for their families or selling them to local taverns or hotels, which vied for the distinction of having "the best coot stews in town." Ironically, according to many recipes of the day, even "the best coot stew" was among the most unpalatable meals in town. For example, a *Field & Stream* recipe from 1924 said to "take the goodly coot and nail it firmly to a hardwood board. Put the board in the sun for about a week. At the end of that time, carefully remove the coot from the board, throw away the coot and cook the board." Other recipes say to boil a coot with potatoes and carrots for a few hours, throw in an old shoe, remove the coot and eat the shoe. Edward Howe Forbush stated in his *Birds of Massachusetts and Other New England States* that "the younger birds have been found quite palatable, if skinned and dressed at once," but "if allowed to hang long with the viscera unremoved, they become vile. I recall a case where a lady cooked such a bird, thereby driving everybody out of the house. She had to throw away both bird and kettle." The reason that coots tasted so bad in a stew is that as they're bottom-feeding birds, they tended to be very oily. When they were cooked in a stew, they become saturated in those oils.

But the Clapp boys—Everett, William and Richard—and the Henderson party—Fred and Bert Henderson, Albert Tilden, George Ford and George Webster—weren't worried at all about debating the pros and cons of the taste of a stewed coot on November 26, 1898. Thanksgiving had just come and gone, and the holiday weekend was still young. There was plenty of time for innocent revelry in the magnificence of the season on the river, and certainly plenty of hunting to be done.

George Woodman, a Trouant's Island resident, visited the Henderson shanty behind Fourth Cliff that afternoon, hoping to score a bird for Sunday dinner, but found that one of the boys had already left for home with the day's prizes, and that Webster was looking to leave as well. The other three boys stayed in the camp, a decision that would cost them dearly as the storm closed in on the South Shore, for as the storm grew, the waters of the North River rose.

The Point Allerton crew saved the crew of the *Henry R. Tilton* by breeches buoy during the Portland Gale. *Courtesy of the Hull Historical Society.*

At the Gurnet, as the sun set, Keeper Rogers began a struggle that would last through the night. "Boatroom doors would not stay locked," he wrote in his log, "had to make them fast with rope." By 7:37 p.m., snow began to fall, and by 11:30 the wind speed had reached seventy-two miles per hour. By 12:00 a.m., the storm that would forever be known as the Portland Gale raged with all its fury.

But the disasters that would define the storm began before the clock struck midnight. At 11 p.m., Consolidated Coal Company's Barge #4, anchored off Hull's Point Allerton Bar, parted from its mooring and began to blow toward Toddy Rocks to the southwest. Shortly after the tug *Cumberland* had left its barge to ride out the storm, Captain Charles Abergh blew four short blasts on his whistle three times to call the tug back, but garnered no response. He would have continued to blow for help had the seas not endangered his ship's fires.

At midnight, watches set out from the South Shore stations. Surfman Fred Eaton of Brant Rock marched southward through the maelstrom to find his Gurnet counterpart, Surfman Nelson King, halfway between the stations. Twenty-three-year-old Thomas Harris, in just his second year as a lifesaver, took the north patrol out of Brant Rock. Surfman Fernando Bearse of Point Allerton set out to the west of his station, heading for Pemberton Point, walking directly into the northeast winds when setting out on his return journey to Stony Beach at 2:00 a.m.

An hour later, Bearse spotted a three-masted schooner a quarter of a mile out from the station. As the surf was pounding so heavily and the wind was blowing so hard, Keeper James decided against launching a boat at that time. About an hour later the vessel had been swept a third of a mile westward, and within about five hundred yards of the shore.

Around 5:00 a.m., just before dawn, and away from the view of the Hull lifesavers, who were then preparing to head out to save the crew of the schooner, Barge #4 crashed on shore in a cacophony of howling wind, roaring surf and screams of dying men. When the boat struck, engineer Charles Nelson and two crewmen simply known as Alfred and Fred disappeared beneath the ocean's frothy surface. Disoriented by the darkness, and battered about relentlessly by the surf, they would never be seen alive again.

Captain Abergh and his steward, John Vanderveer of Baltimore, survived the disaster. Hugging the base of the cliff below Battery Heights (in front of the Jacobs School), they hurriedly and blindly stumbled westward along the shore, soaked by the breaking surf, until they reached a small cottage. Pounding on the door and hollering above the din of the storm, they alerted the owner, Amber Cleverly, who hastened to let them in. They had barely begun to warm themselves in front of the fire before the entire house tilted on its foundation. Gathering his family and the stranded sailors, Cleverly led them all to the annex of the nearby Pemberton Inn. Moments after they arrived, the annex filled up with water and they all had to climb the stairs to the second floor.

At daybreak, around 6:30 a.m., the three-masted schooner, now recognized as the *Henry R. Tilton*, had come within range of the station's Lyle gun. Volunteer lifesavers from the Humane Society—volunteers Osceola and Francis James, Eben Pope, Louis and Joseph Galiano, William Mitchell and John Knowles—joined the Point Allerton crew and other local, unaffiliated men on the way to the wreck. The local Methodist pastor even came out to help, supplying coffee to the would-be lifesavers on the beach, one of whom was his son.

Keeper James landed two shots across the schooner, but one fouled in the debris in the water and another fell out of reach of the enfeebled sailors. A third landed within a reasonable distance and they secured the whip line to the foremast twenty feet above the deck. After bringing the first man ashore, the keeper and his men realized that due to the fact that the vessel was still drifting shoreward, they would have to reset the lines and make them taut again after each rescue. Also, in order to keep the lines clear of debris, the men handling the lines had to stand dangerously close to the breaking waves, and from time to time the sea would engulf the surfmen and their equipment. It took longer than three hours, but the mixed crew of the government's hired men and the town's volunteers brought all seven mariners aboard—Captain H.S. Cobb, mate Frank Randlett and crew Henry Henderson, Charles Colson, L.M. Keane, William Healsley and John Hanson—to safety.

Elsewhere on the South Shore, the lifesavers were hard at work. The North Scituate crew kept patrolling throughout the day in a thick, wet snow and vicious wind. At Fourth Cliff, the surfmen patrolled as far as they could in each direction, but had to stop before reaching their key posts, as, wrote Keeper Fred Stanley, "there was a large quantity of wreckage washing ashore all day." The Clapp boys, who had been warned away from their gunning hut, fled for the safety of their small dory as the depth of the water steadily increased, but abandoned that when a runaway gundalow, a low, flat boat used in salt-haying, happened by. Luckily, it headed for shore in Marshfield, but not before passing within hearing distance of the screams of the Henderson boys, who were being swept away uncontrollably in their own dory.

Surfman Walter Kezer of the Gurnet, a new man hired on October 20, had similar problems. He had to abandon portions of his northward patrol on Duxbury Beach as the sea washed over it and into the bay. Finding a gunner's hut, he burst inside to find some late-staying hunters under assault from the rising waters, with three feet of it already inside their building. He helped them collect their belongings and head for higher ground. Northward, at Brant Rock, high drama was unfolding.

At 8:00 a.m., Surfman Benjamin Simmons set out on the north patrol, but could only walk for about one mile before he was stopped cold by a deep cut in the beach. The same happened to temporary Surfman Arthur Manter, who wasn't even supposed to be working on this day, on the south patrol. Simmons found two men, two women and a child in need of assistance and helped get them to safer ground. Keeper Manter sent Surfman Fred Eaton out to aid his temporary surfman in collecting the station's dory from Green Harbor.

Meanwhile, Keeper Manter took Surfmen Albertus Cahoon and Thomas Harris with him to aid the people of the local village. Together they hurried the residents of Brant Rock into both the lifesaving station and the stone chapel across Ocean Street. "A line was run from the station to the chapel," according to Manter's log. "4 women, 6 children, and 8 men stayed in the station and were provided with dry clothing from the Woman's National Relief Association's supply and stimulants from the medicine chest. We helped about 30 people altogether."

One of the local residents who sought relief at the station, Carrie Phillips, wrote a letter to a friend just days after the storm.

> At 8 a.m. Sunday the breakwater gave away and seas broke through on to the street. At 8:30 the street was full of water, and H. [Henry] said Mr. Bryant's family had gone to the church and I must get the children dressed to go. So the men took Mr. C's three little ones, Mr. Landry's two, and my two little ones to the Church; also Mr. Peterson's two youngest. It was all they could do to get there. Then Leslie Peterson and Henry took me.

The walk to the station proved nearly injurious. Phillips continued,

> We had to dodge piazza roofs and boards, for they were flying through the air. I wanted to get to the church where the children and nearly all the women were, but we had to stop at the life saving station and be thankful to get there. Just as we landed on the station steps Briggs' house sailed away. We went into the station and I thought I was wet and uncomfortable then but it was nothing compared to what I got later on.

At 10:00 a.m., the operation to secure the safety of the people gathering at the station was suddenly and terrifyingly interrupted. Phillips wrote, "We had only been in the station a few minutes when Mr. Cahoon's house and one of the stations hands' houses went down with 'Clifton' the second house from the station next to Melrose. Mrs. Cahoon just escaped with her four children, the youngest five months old. They only had what clothing they had on." Minutes later, the rugged boat room doors, directly facing

The storm had the strength to knock houses off foundations and into Straits Pond in Hull. *Courtesy of the Hull Historical Society.*

the sea to the east, broke loose and allowed the crashing waves to penetrate the building. Thinking quickly, Manter and his men broke down the doors on the opposite end of the room, allowing the water to pass directly through, an effort that Phillips claimed saved them all. The windows in the dining room shattered under the attack, as rocks and stones flew into the station, tossed by the sea. The women and children jumped onto the table and chairs. "The base and legs of the Irvin heater were broken and the table and some dishes were destroyed," wrote Manter. "At this time all the lower part of the station was flooded. The east side of the station and outbuilding were stripped of shingles and some are gone from the north end." Manter estimated that fifty to seventy-five tons of stones had been thrown into the building.

Phillips continued,

> *They did not dare for us to go up stairs. They ran a line over to the church and fastened it to the stone porch thinking we might get over on that, but Mr. Harris, who carried it over, nearly lost his life getting back. The rope slackened up and the rocks knocked his feet from under him and the rope got around his neck. Henry and Baker went to his rescue. So you see what danger there was to get into the street and off your feet. They ran the life boat out and strapped life preservers on to us, even to the little baby.*

Back at the Point Allerton station, Keeper James's wife, Louisa, and the wives of the other surfmen had laid out blankets and hot drinks to care for the survivors of the *Tilton*. Seated in front of a roaring fire in the mess room, the seven sailors finally felt safe for the first time in about fifteen hours.

The same could not be said for several other ships' crews. Almost two hours earlier, at 9:00 a.m., the coal barges *Virginia* and *Lucy R. Nichols* tore from their anchorage off Nantasket Beach, having been left by their tug, *Underwriter*, to ride out the gale. The *Virginia* broke apart and succumbed to Neptune's call, with all aboard perishing. As the *Nichols* blew toward Black Rock at Stony (or Crescent) Beach, on the Hull-Cohasset border, Captain John Petersen and an anonymous crewman leapt overboard, taking their chances with the sea, which made sure they would never walk the earth again.

In probably the most amazing instance of pure luck throughout the entire span of the storm, a mast from the disintegrating *Nichols* fell directly across to the small island at Black Rock, creating an extremely temporary walkway to safety for the remaining crew members. The three men—John Soderstrom, B. Fray and Oscar Colson—dashed across the mast toward the only available shelter, a gunning hut, as the sea swallowed their vessel behind them. They entered the hut, built a fire and waited.

Somewhere off of Hull's shores the *Minnie Stowe, Abel E. Babcock, James H. Hoyt, Baltimore* and countless other vessels disappeared without witnesses.

By the time Joshua and his lifesavers had finished with their rescue efforts on the *Tilton*, word had already arrived that Consolidated Coal Company's Barge #1 was dragging ashore on Toddy Rocks, three-quarters of a mile to the west. Knowing it would be impossible to drag their second beach apparatus to the scene of the wreck due to the tangled masses of telephone, telegraph and electrical wiring in front of Point Allerton station, Keeper James conferred with his son, Osceola, who agreed to send some of his men back for the Massachusetts Humane Society's Hunt gun at Station #18, on Stony Beach. Osceola hired a team of horses to bring back the equipment, as the rest of the lifesavers headed for the wreck.

The two crews reached Barge #1 about 11:00 a.m. and set up the Humane Society's beach apparatus. They fired shots with the Hunt gun before realizing that the barge was about to break into pieces. Both keepers, Joshua and Osceola, called for volunteers to wade out into the surf. Tying lines around their waists, a group of surfmen walked out among the wreckage as far as they could, getting as close to the distressed vessel as possible, trusting their friends on the beach to drag them to safety at the first sign of real danger. Within moments the pilothouse broke off the barge and began riding the waves toward the shore. With a tremendous crash it slammed to earth heavily, tossing its passengers into a pile on the beach. The lifesavers in the surf rushed to grab the men before the undertow dragged them back in again. The surfmen held onto the sailors and waited for the next wave to crash, which carried them all to a point on the beach where they could scramble to safety. As the wave hit, though, a flying piece of debris struck the leg of volunteer Louis F. Galiano, leaving a deep bone bruise. His heroic rescue work during the Portland Gale ended there and then.

Knowing it would be impossible to bring the survivors back to the station into the driving northeast winds, Joshua looked for the nearest available shelter. He spotted a cottage nearby and banged on the door, but the family had fled. He and his men then crashed down the door, dragging in the helpless forms from the wreck. The crew made a fire, stripped off all of the sailors' wet clothing and wrapped them in any quilts and blankets they could find. One of the surfmen found the liquor cabinet and heated up some whiskey drinks to warm the survivors from the inside.

As he came to his senses, the master of the barge, Captain Joshua Thomas, started to violently curse the master of the tug, claiming that his crew and the crew of Barge #4 had been left to die. This mention was the first the lifesavers had heard of the #4.

Finally back at the station in the afternoon, Joshua James spotted a schooner ashore of Great Brewster Island, and knew that there was no way he could launch a boat into such powerful seas. He decided to wait until the surf quieted. As the storm continued to rage, the keeper feared that the night's high tide would be even worse than the morning's, an unbelievable thought, as Hull Village had by then become a white-capped lake. Down the street from the station, a man could be seen waving his arms frantically through his chamber window. Surfman #1, George F. Pope, Joshua's nephew, launched a dory onto the flooded street and rowed to the man's rescue, bringing him to higher ground. That afternoon, after receiving word from the Pemberton Hotel of the presence of the Cleverly family and the crew of Barge #4, the keeper sent a team of horses to retrieve them and bring them to the lifesaving station. By mid-afternoon the wives of the surfmen were caring for fourteen wet, cold, tired mariners, as well as the Cleverly family.

While the Hull men fought to save the Barge #1 crew, the Brant Rock crew responded to another call. Keeper Manter wrote,

> *About 11.30 a.m. Lloyd Peterson, a resident of Brant Rock, reported to me that a schooner was ashore about ½ mile south of the station and the crew of 8 men were in a cottage near the wreck. I at once sent the surfmen to the place to help the men to the station and furnished them with dry clothing from the Woman's National Relief Association's supply. As the station was uninhabitable they returned to the cottage until the next day when they came to the station and were cared for three days.*

Surfmen Eaton, Manter and Simmons returned to the Brant Rock station around 1:00 p.m., shocked to see what had happened to the first floor of their building. At Fourth Cliff, Keeper Stanley reported, "During the gale this day the flagpole was blown, the out-building was moved off from its foundation and a lot of shingles torn off and the platforms were washed away with the slats of the Station and a key post with one Key." His son, Surfman Thomas P. Stanley of the Gurnet crew, patrolled Duxbury Beach between 12:00 and 4:00 p.m., but reported that no surfman from Brant Rock had met him along the way. To the west of the Gurnet Point station, the key post on Saquish Beach had also washed away, as had a portion of the old 1874 station.

"As soon as tide left so that we could go," wrote Keeper Rogers, "the west patrol sent a man that way, met the Capt. of the *Venus*, who said his sloop was ashore in Saquish

The *Edgar S. Foster* came ashore at Brant Rock. *Courtesy of Richard Boonisar.*

cove." All hands from the *Venus* were safe, but the captain noted that of the eleven ships anchored between Saquish and Clark's Island on Saturday night, only two were now visible: his and the *Charles J. Parker*, which had lost both masts. "I asked him if there was anything we could do for him," Rogers recounted, adding, "he said 'no living man could do anything on the water on a day like this.'"

More news, though, was forthcoming. Rogers wrote,

> *The Surfman from the west returned* [and he] *stated that he could not see any thing on account of the snow, but said that the gunners there told him the Sch. seemed to be riding all right the last time they saw her. In the mean time an unknown Sch. was sighted at anchor about ½ mile ENE from Gurnet head, and being in a very dangerous place, all hands kept watch of her until night set in, then placed two men on watch, but she did not use any light, so that was the last we saw of her.*

The human drama of the storm continued to unfold at the Brant Rock station. "At 2 p.m. William Jones and Alger Brown reported at the station that a schooner was stranded about 2 miles north of the station and there were two dead men on the schooner's deck and one on the shore," noted Manter. "I at once sent Surfmen T.W. Baker and B.F. Simmons to the scene with orders to move the bodies above the reach of the tide. I notified the undertaker at Marshfield who took charge of them the next morning. The nine survivors were cared for at a farmhouse near the wreck." With night rapidly approaching and the fear of the evening's high tide being worse than that of the morning, Manter began preparations to care for the souls gathered unwittingly into his care at the station. "All of the station blankets and pillows and some station wood were taken to the chapel. There were 28 people, including the station crew, who stayed in the chapel through the night. The patrol was not maintained during the night because the crew were so exhausted from the unusual hard work of the day."

In North Scituate, Keeper Brown told his crews to remain at the station instead of patrolling at 4:00 and 8:00 p.m., fearing for their safety with the tremendous amount of wreckage floating in the surf and strewn across the beaches. At Fourth Cliff, patrolling to the north was no longer an option. "The beach a little north of this Cliff is cut through so that it is impossible to get across except with a boat and then only occasionally," wrote Keeper Stanley. The North River, in combination with the storm, had destroyed the barrier beach that had tenuously held Third and Fourth Cliffs together for centuries.

The storm had spent its fury by the next high tide, around 10:30 p.m. At Point Allerton, Keeper James sent his men on patrol that night, although both of the station's key posts had washed away and the beaches were nearly impassable with wreckage. At Little Brewster Island, the crew of the schooner *Calvin F. Baker*, stranded on the island since 3:00 a.m. on Sunday, November 27, had clambered into the rigging as the aft deck crumbled beneath their feet. During the night, their pitiful cries for help kept Keeper Henry Pingree's wife awake in a state of horror, the stress of which would eventually kill her. Fifty-seven-year-old First Mate Burgess Howland lost his strength in the freezing cold and dropped into the ocean, dead. Soon thereafter, Second Mate R. McIsaacs met the same fate. Steward Willis H. Studley froze to death in place.

At 1:00 a.m. on Monday, November 28, Keeper Brown at North Scituate deemed it safe to set his men back on their patrols, safety being a relative term. By his definition, the fact that the seas were no longer washing over the entirety of the beach made it safe.

Three hours later the south patrolman returned to the station to report that a well-known pilot boat, the *Columbia*, "was ashore on top of the beach with both masts gone and no one there. I took three of the crew and went down to her. They told me there was no one left but they found one body in the hole," wrote Brown. "We picked one body up when we went down and saw one in the surf but could not get it." Brown sent two members of the crew to the site of the wreck at the northern end of Cedar Point, and relieved them with three men a few hours later. The five men of the *Columbia* had all perished, and the remaining bodies eventually appeared in the still rough waters. "They saw them in the surf but couldn't get them," said Brown.

At first light the next morning, Keeper James used his glass to look out to Boston Light on Little Brewster Island for a predetermined distress signal agreed upon by himself and light keeper Pingree. Seeing it, the USLSS crew and four volunteers launched Massachusetts Humane Society surfboat #17, *Boston Herald* (the only other Humane Society boat built along the same lines as the famous surfboat *Nantasket*), from Stony Beach and headed for the wreck. Spotting the tug *Ariel*, the captain arranged to be pulled as close as they could to Great Brewster Island, resting the weary arms of the mixed crew.

When the crew of the tug dared go no farther, the surfmen began to row. Passing through a series of breakers, the rescuers finally settled alongside the vessel the *Calvin*

F. Baker and brought what was left of its crew to safety. Five men had survived to tell their tale. Two of Captain Magathlin's men were none the worse for their ordeal, yet two had badly swollen and frostbitten feet. Prying the dead steward from the rigging, the lifesavers brought the victims to the tug, where the captain had hot whiskey waiting.

After being pulled back to Stony Beach by the tug, the crew headed to the station. The five survivors entered the already-overcrowded building and sat down before the fire to thaw themselves, bringing the total of "lucky ones" to nineteen. As the crew brought the frozen steward to the morgue, they wondered just how many sailors had not been so lucky in the past two days.

As the crew of the Point Allerton completed their grisly task, Keeper Stanley and the Fourth Cliff crew "spent the day in clearing away the wreckage about the premises and looking for any bodies that might come ashore."

At Brant Rock, stated Keeper Manter, "early in the morning we commenced to clear the dining room and kitchen of stone, etc. We were obliged to take our breakfast and dinners in the chapel, on account of the station being in such a bad condition."

To the south, at Gurnet Point, Keeper Rogers sent Surfmen Wixon, King and Edward Tobin to Saquish to board the schooner *Charles W. Parker*, which had survived the worst of the storm, even with the loss of its masts. A tugboat from Plymouth arrived and towed the vessel into the harbor. Surfman Stanley, meanwhile, headed for Duxbury with the station's mail. On his return he found a dead body floating in the surf, but was unable to haul it ashore. The undertow proved to be his match in strength. He returned to the station with the news, and the entire crew headed out onto the beach to retrieve it. They lost track of it, and it was never found again. Rogers also noted that the day's high tide washed away two small boats the crew had pulled to safety for local residents, and that the gunners who had come to the station for safety had left for home.

At 4:00 p.m., reported Keeper Manter at Brant Rock, "Daniel Graffam, a resident of Green Harbor village, came to the station and informed me that he had found a body on Duxbury beach and had moved it beyond the reach of the tide and covered it up. I at once notified the undertaker at Marshfield who took charge of it." Brant Rock crews began patrolling again at sunset on Monday night.

In Hull, Keeper James and the weary men of the town had one more challenge to face. Stepping back into the lifesaving station around 10:30 a.m., the keeper received news from Alfred Galiano that a group of what looked to be five men had set up a distress signal at Black Rock, six miles to the south-southeast. James again hailed his son Osceola, and together the surfmen and the volunteers headed for the Bayside Humane Society boathouse to collect the trusty surfboat *Nantasket*.

Already responding to the signal, Cohasset's Humane Society volunteers—Captain William Brennock, Albert Brennock, John Fratus, Allie Morris, Frank Martin, Joseph J. and Joseph E. Grassie, Manuel Antone and Frank Salvador—attempted to launch from Stony Beach, only to have their boat capsize a few feet from shore. Struggling back up the beach, they headed for the summer home of George Swallow of the governor's council, where caretaker Arthur Mulvey tended to their needs.

The *Mertis H. Perry* claimed five lives at Rexhame. *Courtesy of Richard Boonisar.*

Keeper James and his crew decided to launch *Nantasket* from protected Gun Rock Cove, about a mile north of Black Rock, after waiting almost an hour for the seas to abate. They pulled out to the island, rowing with the wind, but had to wait for longer than an hour to make a safe landing. On the island they could see a small gunning hut.

Inside the hut huddled three men, sailors from the coal schooner *Lucy A. Nichols*. One man complained of a broken shoulder and showed several contusions about the head and legs. Just before sundown the crew launched *Nantasket* once again, rowing for a mile headlong into a heavy north-northwest wind. Once on shore, Joshua James hired a team to go ahead and call for a doctor to meet them at the station. At 7:00 p.m., the crew finally returned to the station for the night. There, twenty-two survivors from five different vessels found comfort, thanks to the tireless efforts of the women of the town. On Monday night, Keeper James finally told his men to stand down. "The weather looking favorable this evening the men were exempt from Patrol to take rest after the heavy strain since 12 o'clock Saturday night."

Surfman Tobin from the Gurnet walked the 8:00 p.m. to 12:00 a.m. patrol to the north, but never made contact with a Brant Rock surfman, so he continued on to the station. Being thoroughly exhausted, he spent the night there instead of walking home.

Tuesday morning, the Brant Rock crew returned to their task of removing the stones from their boat room, and did their best to get their lifesaving gear back into working order. Surfman Tobin left at first light for the Gurnet. Four men from the Fourth Cliff crew joined the locals in searching for the bodies of the Henderson brothers and Albert

Coal barges along Hull's shores dropped fifteen thousand tons of the fuel on the seafloor, of which eleven thousand tons washed ashore. *Courtesy of the Hull Historical Society.*

Tilden, last seen careening helplessly down the North River on Sunday. The rest of the crew watched the beach for any other dead bodies that might come ashore.

At the Gurnet, Keeper Rogers took his men down to examine the old station, which was still being used as a boathouse. It was worse off up close than at first glance, and the crew could not entirely tell what was missing. They noted that the upper floor had settled about three feet, and that everything on the lower floor except for the boats themselves had washed away. They figured that on a normal high tide, water would now enter the building.

Meanwhile, Surfman Tobin returned to the station with news of another dead body, lying just about where the station's key post once stood. Seaweed and sand had conspired to keep the body in the ground, making it impossible for Tobin to pull it out alone. Rogers and Surfman King joined Tobin on the way back, harnessing up a horse and wagon. Together they dislodged the body from the wet sand as the tide rushed in around it. "Found the head badly bruised, should say it had been dead surely 24 hours," wrote Rogers. "We then rolled the body in one of Station blankets, put it in the team, returned to station, took Monomoy surf-boat and all of crew except Tobin, went to Town and delivered body to coroner E.O. Hill, Plymouth."

For the official log—according to the *Revised Regulations of the United States Life-Saving Service*, the responsibility for identification of such victims of the sea belonged to the keeper—Rogers described the body: "He had black hair, none on top of head. Blue eyes, 5 ft 8½ inches tall. One joint of the finger next to little finger gone, on right hand. Blue pants. Light woolen drawers, white. Nothing on body except Oil Jacket which was hauled over his head. Blue mixed woolen stockings, with white toes. Russet lace shoes. Black mustache."

Six members of the crew of the schooner *Venus*, still ashore on Saquish Beach, arrived at the Gurnet Point station requesting shelter, food and beds, which Rogers and his crew provided.

That same morning, the *Boston Herald* reported the loss of the side-wheel steamship *Portland*, of the Boston to Portland run. Captain Hollis H. Blanchard, most likely figuring he could outrun the oncoming storm, had pulled the boat away from Boston's India Wharf at precisely 7:00 p.m. on Saturday, November 26, a decision that proved to be fatal to the (at latest estimation) 192 passengers and crew members aboard. Twenty-four hours later, wreckage clearly identifiable as having belonged to the *Portland* washed ashore on Cape Cod.

From the cupola atop the Point Allerton station, Keeper James and his tired surfmen held a commanding panoramic view of the devastation in Boston Harbor. Dozens of vessels rested eerily silent on the shores of Thompson's, Spectacle, Rainsford and Moon Islands in the inner harbor. The barge *Grant* had stranded on Gallop's, while the schooners *G.M. Hopkins*, *John S. Ames* and *Lizzie Dyas* had found final resting places on or near George's.

Twelve corpses washed ashore in Hull in the first few days after the storm. Walking the lonely lane down to the town dead house, Keeper James did his best to match descriptive letters sent by mourning relatives to tattoos, scars and missing teeth.

Some bodies yielded very few clues. "Thursday morning the body of one of the shipwrecked sailors was picked up on Nantasket Beach in a perfectly nude condition with the exception of a belt about his waist. On one finger he had a silver ring. He was evidently a Swede about 30 years old." Others easily gave up their identities, according to the report of the *Hull Beacon* weekly newspaper:

> One of the bodies was that of a man 5 feet 9 inches in hight [sic], weighing about 175 pounds. His hair and mustache were sandy. On the inside of the right forearm, in india ink, there was a woman resting on a table, hand shading eyes, in left hand basket of fruit. The work is well executed. The woman is fancifully attired, the design being decidedly Parisian. Around the right wrist there is also a bracelet in india ink, connecting with a wreath on the inside of it, in which there is a woman's head.
>
> In one of the pockets the searchers found a letter addressed to "Mr. W.W. Phillips, 33 North 2nd St., Camden, N.J."
>
> The front of the envelope bears the following postmark, "Philadelphia, Penn., Nov. 4, 7.30 p.m., '98."
>
> On the back of the envelope is the reception postmark: "Camden, Nov. 5, 6 a.m., 1898, N.J."
>
> The letter is simply dated Friday, 1.30, and is addressed to "Dear Weston," which would correspond with one of the first initials on the envelope. The contents of the epistle is of a character that precludes any doubt that it belonged to any person than the one on which it was found. It bears only the signature of "Mattie." Persons bearing the following names are referred to in it: "Sophie," "Clara," "Will," "Mom," and "Mr. Kerns."

The *Abel E. Babcock* crew was lost during the storm. All that came ashore was the wreckage of their ship. *Courtesy of the Hull Historical Society.*

Using such evidence, in some cases more and in some cases less, James identified four of the twelve bodies. The town buried the rest at Strangers Corner, a mass unmarked grave of nearly one hundred unknown sailors at the Hull Village Cemetery. The horrible, undignified manner in which shipwreck victims spent their final hours above ground in Hull—no caskets, no embalming—inspired local newspaper editor Floretta Vining to push for the appointment of a town undertaker and the construction of a receiving tomb for storage of dead bodies until positively identified.

As if wrestling with such a horrible chore were not enough to wear down his resolve, Keeper James also had to face the hopeful families of the crew of the schooner *Abel E. Babcock,* who had read in one of the Boston papers that the men of Hull had heroically pulled their loved ones to safety, and had come to the Point Allerton station to collect them. He could only report that the bow of the vessel had been found, and nothing else. Heartbroken, the now-grieving families left for home. Two days after the storm, Joshua also learned that one of his lifelong friends and the man who led his first lifeboat rescue, Moses Binney Tower, had died at his home in Auburndale at age eighty-four. Overburdened with his duties, James never got the chance to say goodbye.

Over the next week, the Life-Saving Service crews rebuilt their stations and their lives. At the Gurnet, Keeper Rogers found that two navigational buoys, the whistling buoy off the Gurnet and the number six buoy off Duxbury Beach's High Pines area, had been blown well off station. He contacted the Lighthouse Service with the news. In the meantime, his crew worked at transferring everything from the old station into the "new" station, as, he said, "things were not safe there, the next storm will take it away, if a hard blow does not." The crew finally could account for missing items: nine oars, old shot lines, seven paintbrushes, two skids and a tally board had gone missing. The station dory proved to have a hole in it, and the gap in the rocks that the crew had historically used to launch boats had to be cleared out. On December 3, Rogers learned from the Plymouth police that the body delivered to them several days earlier had still not been identified.

Frustratingly, the number six check from the Gurnet Point station had vanished. Recounting the steps of the past week, Rogers traced it back to the Brant Rock station on Saturday, November 26, when Surfman Kezer had reached that station on patrol. Keeper Manter at Brant Rock promised to turn his station upside down until he found it.

Assistant Inspector of Life-Saving Stations Worth G. Ross arrived at Brant Rock on November 30 to assess the damage to the building, joined a few days later by the service's assistant superintendent of construction, Andre Fourchy. The crew continued to work from sunup until sundown removing the stones from the boat room. They tossed their last one out on December 3. They resumed their patrols as usual, stopped from meeting their Gurnet brethren due to a deep cut on the beach. "The patrolmen will not be able to meet on the high water for a time," wrote Manter.

On December 6, an eerie sight appeared a mile east-southeast of the Brant Rock station: a dismasted schooner gliding silently toward the coast. Keeper Manter and his men launched their surfboat and pulled toward the ghost ship, the *Grace*, finding her devoid of human life. The ship had been reported lost off Cape Cod on November 27 and, waterlogged and abandoned, "Her deck and house are gone and she is nothing but a shell," wrote Manter. "I have informed a brother in law of the Capt the condition of the Sch as it is supposed the Capt and two sons were lost."

At Point Allerton, the crew responded to a false report that a three-masted schooner was coming ashore four miles to the south on Nantasket Beach on November 30 during a thick snowstorm. They left the station at 9:30 a.m., returning at 3:00 p.m. On December 1, the survivors of the wrecks of the schooners *Henry R. Tilton* and *Calvin F. Baker* and the barge *Lucy Nichols* left the station. The next morning, Keeper James reported, "The supply of men's clothing provided this station from the WNRA has been expended." On December 3, the crew found their key posts amongst the wreckage on the beaches and put them back in place.

On December 5, Surfman Francis Mitchell found the body of the captain of the barge *Lucy Nichols*; on December 6, the crew picked up the body of the mate. For the next week, the crew worked at clearing the grounds of the station from all the "wreckage, rocks, gravel, &c," and on December 12, Assistant Inspector Ross came to see how the building had held up during the storm. He left them with instructions to repair their launch way, erect their flagpole and return their station to working order. On December 18, Keeper James took his crew out in their surfboat for a row among the Boston Harbor Islands, three weeks after the storm, to make one final sweep for dead bodies. They found none.

One week after the storm, on Sunday, December 4, Keeper James and his Point Allerton crew had been jolted from their station by a horrible cry just outside their doors, dashing out into the blackness of night with lanterns in hand, foraying through both the duck pond behind the station and then onto the beach across the way. After an extended search, they concluded that either they had better prepare to look for a body at daylight, or that they had been given a false alarm. Neither case proved to be true. The "unearthly and blood-curdling" scream that they had heard actually came from a passing admirer on horseback, young James Cashman, who offered his salute to his heroes on his way by. "Now don't laugh at the life savers," wrote the *Hull Beacon* of December 10. "This incident shows how prompt and faithful they are to respond to every cry. Since their fearful experience in the late storm the very atmosphere is haunted with distress cries."

From Point Allerton to the Gurnet, from Hull to Plymouth, the men of the U.S. Life-Saving Service fought the Portland Gale and its aftermath for three full weeks. They rescued many, retrieved the dead bodies of several others and opened the doors of their stations to anybody in need during the one weather event that even the old-timers had to admit rivaled the Minot's Light Gale of 1851. With aching arms, shoulders and backs, burning leg muscles and exhausted minds, they looked toward the turn of the year with an earnest expectation for better days. After all, they had lived through the storm of the century.

Or so they hoped.

ALL THAT'S LEFT

The Life-Saving Service ceased to be on January 28, 1915, when President Woodrow Wilson signed the act that created the Coast Guard. The act did not abolish the service, but instead merged it with its old overseeing agency, the Revenue Cutter Service, under the new name. Operationally, not much changed immediately for the members of the South Shore stations. They still walked patrols at night and still responded to shipwrecks in small, exposed boats. A layer of bureaucracy had been added to their lives, and their once more civilian than military organization was now quasi military. In time, keepers would become warrant officers, although some decided to retire right away. For some surfmen and keepers who had worked for the Life-Saving Service into their sixties because they could not afford not to be working, the sudden access to a pension was all the encouragement they needed to hang up their kerosene lanterns and oil slickers for good.

As for their volunteer counterparts on the South Shore, the Humane Society lifesavers kept themselves available for rescue duty for several more years, although the need for their services was fading fast. Motor lifeboats had been tested in Marquette, Michigan, in 1899, and by 1907 were in use at many Life-Saving Service stations around the country. Such craft cut down Life-Saving Service boat crew sizes, allowed for larger gaps along the coast between stations and pulled the remaining crews away from their traditional shorefront stations. To properly house and launch such boats, the Life-Saving Service needed stations on protected coves, rather than across from the pounding surf. Stations added off-site boathouses or were moved entirely. The quick response capability of the Life-Saving Service's and then the Coast Guard's motor lifeboats led to the slow disappearance of the Humane Society lifesavers. In a symbolic effort, a year before he died, Osceola James, Joshua's son, led the volunteer rescue of the crew of the five-masted schooner *Nancy* off Nantasket Beach on February 19, 1927. For the rescue, Osceola and his crew pulled out the surfboat-lifeboat *Nantasket* for one final run. In the 1930s, *Nantasket* headed south to the Mariners Museum in Newport News, Virginia, to be saved as a relic of the region's lifesaving history.

By the 1970s, the home that Joshua James built, the Point Allerton Life-Saving Station, had seen better days. The station itself needed to be rescued. *Courtesy of the National Archives and Records Administration.*

The building had undergone several renovations through the years, including the removal of both the boat room doors and the cupola. They since have been replaced by the hard work of the Hull Lifesaving Museum. *Courtesy of the National Archives and Records Administration.*

The successful development of the motor lifeboat was only one change that affected the way that America's lifesavers approached their jobs. The first ship-to-shore telegraphed SOS (or, more accurately, "CDQ") sounded on January 23, 1909, when the RMS *Republic* and the Italian liner *Florida* collided southwest of the Nantucket lightship. Where once lifesavers had to look through snow and fog for flags flying upside down in a ship's rigging or for other signals that a ship was in the direst of consequences, Morse code now tore through the air. Where once mariners on those ships looked to the shore for flares to fire into the sky, they instead turned to their radio shacks for incoming dots and dashes to give them instructions.

The men of the Coast Guard continued traditional beach patrols for several decades, even as their reputations took hits, thanks to their ever evolving mission load. Until 1920, they were still revered as storm fighters, men who risked their lives so others might live. Prohibition changed all that. Men who days earlier had been hailed as heroes became enemies of the public, or at least that portion of the public that wanted a sip of alcohol from time to time. They still patrolled the beaches, but those patrols became ever more dangerous. Coast Guardsmen caught unaware by rumrunners unloading their contraband were susceptible to and sometimes succumbed to kidnappings and even beatings. And although it would take a while for Coast Guardsmen to earn their respect once again, the American people turned to them as a first line of defense against enemy attack in World War II. Coast Guardsman John Cullen, patrolling from the Amagansett Coast Guard Station on Long Island, New York, on June 12, 1942, stumbled onto a group of four Nazi spies coming ashore from a U-boat. Knowing he was outnumbered, he pretended to accept a bribe from them to keep quiet and then reported them to authorities as they boarded a train for New York City, leading to their capture. Acts like that one brought the reputation of the Coast Guardsmen back to prominence, if not to where it had once been when their only enemy had been the sea.

Sail was slowly giving way to steam as the main method of propulsion for ships carrying cargo in and out of ports during the first few decades of the twentieth century. The construction of deeper draft vessels meant fewer had to be used to carry the same loads that had always been shipped, and in fact, merchants could now ship more cargo. The days of tugs pulling three or four minimally powered and heavily laden barges were vanishing. The presence of fewer ships meant fewer shipwrecks, and comparatively less work for the service to do in that regard.

In Hull, shipping moved farther from the coast. From the 1600s to 1905, most ships entering the harbor followed the traditional route between Point Allerton and the Brewster Islands, up between Lovell's, Gallops and George's Islands and westward into the port of Boston (which was losing ground to New York as a center of trade, anyway). On September 1, 1905, Graves Lighthouse illuminated the night sky for the first time, marking a new, deeper, straighter, broader channel. President Roads became the approach of choice for ships. The crew at Point Allerton watched their traffic divert northward and for a few short years had to live with the prospect of rowing twice their usual distance to respond to shipwrecks, should northeast winds push vessels against the Graves. They were relieved when motor surfboats and motor lifeboats came into widespread use.

To accommodate those boats, the Life-Saving Service built a boathouse at Pemberton, or Windmill Point, in the shadow of the grand Pemberton Hotel and alongside the steamer dock, just after the beginning of the twentieth century. Bigger boats led to bigger boathouses. The Coast Guard added the boathouse that stands now at Pemberton in the 1930s. Late in that decade, the service contemplated replacing the Point Allerton Life-Saving Station with a Colonial Revival, "Roosevelt-type" station on nearby Gallops Hill. That proposed construction never came to pass, and Coast Guardsmen serving at the Point Allerton station continued to work in the old wooden building until the late 1960s. On April 18, 1970, the Coast Guard commissioned its new facility at the northwestern end of Hull Hill. That station today remains one of the busiest small boat search and rescue stations in the United States.

In 1971, the Coast Guard prepared to dispose of the old station, deeming its days of usefulness in service to the country as having passed. An assessment in August 1971 suggested the station should be sold for $20,000, and that it could best be used as a single-family home. Project Turnabout, a drug rehabilitation organization, moved into

The "Roosevelt-type" Colonial Revival–style station built on First Cliff in Scituate replaced the Fourth Cliff and North Scituate facilities. Today it's the home of the Stellwagen Bank National Marine Sanctuary offices. *Courtesy of the Scituate Historical Society.*

the building in 1972. Beset with financial problems, the organization did not survive. On November 18, 1980, the Town of Hull accepted the station from the General Services Administration for "Historic Monument" purposes. By that time, the Hull Lifesaving Museum movement was already underway.

Four historic structures in Hull remain from the days of wooden lifeboats and ironmen: the Point Allerton Life-Saving Station (now the museum), the Pemberton Point boathouse and one each Humane Society mortar station and boathouse, now private homes, on Stony Beach. The boathouse serves as the physical and spiritual center of the museum's Maritime Program, which teaches today's kids the skills and ethics of the lifesavers of old. The program runs several popular rowing races throughout the calendar year from Hull, and has reached into Boston to help adjudicated youths learn the teamwork values of "pulling together" and literally being "in the same boat."

The Hull Lifesaving Museum stands out as one of the premier facilities of its type in the country. Although the station was altered over time, the Victorian-era ambience lingers, and the days of Joshua James return when one steps onto its ancient wooden floors. The people of Hull collaborated to bring the surfboat-lifeboat *Nantasket* back home in the early 1980s, transported from Virginia aboard a Daley and Wanzer moving truck. This was a fitting move, as that company had its origins in a company called Knight's Express. Knight's was once owned by James Dowd, who also served as a surfman under Joshua James. *Nantasket* is the centerpiece of the museum's expansive collection of Humane Society, Life-Saving Service and Coast Guard artifacts.

The Brant Rock Coast Guard Station remained a vibrant, important part of the Marshfield community through World War II. *Courtesy of Richard Boonisar.*

Deeper in Hull Village, the Hull Historical Society holds a chunk of plaster with the name *Ulrica* and the date December 16, 1896, carved into it, a remnant of that amazing rescue. Out at Stony Beach, the Humane Society's lifeboat and mortar stations are now private homes. In the Hull cemetery, more than fifty lifesavers are buried, including the old keeper himself.

All throughout town, there are signs that Joshua James has not been forgotten: a painting on a sea wall at Stony Beach; Joshua James Park at the base of Allerton Hill at X Street; on the sides of the trucks of the Hull Department of Fire, Rescue and Emergency Services; and on a mural overlooking the town's mini-golf course. And of course his countenance hangs in the current Point Allerton Coast Guard Station. For a while, the Ocean Club Café at the base of Atlantic Hill bore the name Joshua Jaames (using the family's original Dutch spelling) and the Hull Harbormaster's boat carried his name as well. The house in which he lived in Hull Village bears a plaque to that effect on an exterior wall.

The North Scituate Life-Saving Station still stands firmly upon the ground on which it was built, a private residence on Surfside Road. Two other structures from the days of the Life-Saving Service era, both Humane Society boathouses, remain. One stands in the Glades, inaccessible to the general public, while the other, in Scituate Harbor, is exactly the opposite. The Town of Scituate purchased the boatyard on which it sits for public use and restored the building using Community Preservation funds. Plans are to use it as a center for boating safety classes, among other ideas, in the near future.

The Fourth Cliff Life-Saving Station burned down in a fire in 1919 and was never rebuilt. The lot at the southern base of the cliff has never been reused. The "new" mouth of the North River still separates Third and Fourth Cliffs as a living reminder of the Portland Gale of 1898. The remains of a gundalow, a low, wooden salt-haying craft used on the river until the storm's arrival, sit rotting in the marsh behind Fourth Cliff, possibly the one used by the Clapp boys to escape the ravages of the gale alive.

GOVERNMENT SALE
AS SEPARATE ITEMS

COAST GUARD PROPERTIES
GURNET POINT, PLYMOUTH, MASSACHUSETTS

BID OPENING - JUNE 21, 1968
SEALED BIDS INVITED - CASH OR CREDIT

LOCATION AND DESCRIPTION

Bids are invited for the purchase of former Coast Guard properties located at Gurnet Point in Plymouth, Massachusetts. The properties consist of four parcels of land offered as two separate items, described as follows:

ITEM 1 - PARCELS A and D - two parcels of vacant land.
Parcel A is a 6.25 acre tract adjoining the active Coast Guard Station and Light Tower.

Parcel D is a 0.51 of an acre tract located about ½ mile west of Parcel A on Saquish Neck. Most of this parcel is underwater or subject to flooding at high tide.

ITEM 2 - DWELLING AND BOATHOUSE SITES
The Dwelling Site is a 0.25 of an acre lot bounded by four unimproved streets. The dwelling is a 6 room, 2-story, wood frame house, with outside dimensions of about 47' x 36'.

The Boathouse Site is a 0.05 of an acre site located across the street from the dwelling. The boathouse building has two floors, is of wood frame construction and has outside dimensions of about 18' x 32'.

Full particulars on the items, including conditions, reservations and restrictions on transfer, are included in Invitation No. GS-01-DR-(S)-8-0041.

INSPECTION

The property may be inspected on Tuesdays and Fridays between 9:00 A.M. and 3:30 P.M., *by appointment made at least 24 hours in advance.* For appointment, contact Commander, Plymouth Light Station, U. S. Coast Guard, Plymouth, Massachusetts - Telephone: 617 - 934 - 2053.

HOW, WHEN AND WHERE TO BUY

All bids must be submitted on Invitation, Bid and Acceptance Form No. GS-01-DR-(S)-8-0041 which contains complete bidding instructions. Bids will be received at General Services Administration, Room E-111, John Fitzgerald Kennedy Federal Building, Government Center, Boston, Massachusetts 02203, until 11:00 A.M., EDST, June 21, 1968, at which time and place they will be publicly opened and read.

For the required Form No. GS-01-DR-(S)-8-0041 and further information, call or write:

GENERAL SERVICES ADMINISTRATION
PROPERTY MANAGEMENT AND DISPOSAL SERVICE
Post Office & Courthouse, Boston, Massachusetts 02109
Tel. No. 617 - 223-2852

The General Services Administration auctioned off many former lifesaving stations, including the Gurnet Bibb #2 building. The Boonisar family bought it at auction in 1968 and still owns it today. *Courtesy of the National Archives and Records Administration.*

During the local Portland Gale centennial remembrance ceremonies, the people of Humarock, led by resident Russell Clark, dedicated the Sea Street Bridge, stretching from Marshfield's Seaview section over to the peninsula, in memory of Keeper Frederick Stanley. The Scituate Historical Society also marked the site of the loss of the pilot boat *Columbia* with a plaque on a sea wall at the northern convergence of Rebecca and Lighthouse Roads.

The Coast Guard eventually centralized its search and rescue efforts in Scituate at a new station on First Cliff in 1938. The service built new buildings all around the country during the Great Depression in the Colonial Revival style, the most frequently used design known as the "Roosevelt type" for the president then in office. The Scituate station came with a boathouse in the harbor and a four-bay utility building. During World War II, as many as forty Coast Guardsmen worked from the station, but by the mid-1990s a minimal crew remained, as the Coast Guard went through government-mandated "right-sizing." The building had been damaged by a fire in 1984 that destroyed the cupola and two large pavilions had been added, leaving it looking little like the classic Roosevelt-type found elsewhere along the coast (for comparison, another stands on the northeast side of the Cape Cod Canal). For efficiency's sake, the Coast Guard moved out of the First Cliff station and into a new, smaller building on Cole Parkway on the opposite side of the harbor, the unit becoming a seasonal "station-small" under the command of the Point Allerton Coast Guard Station to the north.

The boat room doors that would not stay closed for Augustus Rogers during the Portland Gale give Richard Boonisar the same problems today during storms. *Courtesy of the National Archives and Records Administration.*

The old station entered the General Services Administration disposal process and ended up in the domain of the National Oceanic and Atmospheric Administration. The young Stellwagen Bank National Marine Sanctuary staff had been searching for a new home that offered both office space and a place from which to launch their research vessels. Since taking the building over, NOAA has installed an environmentally friendly geothermal heating unit, converted the old garage over to meeting space and made other significant changes to the old building.

The Coast Guard, under the direction of then–Point Allerton commanding officer Chief Warrant Officer Craig D. Bitler, turned over many of the First Cliff station accoutrements to the Scituate Historical Society; in turn, when the time came to decorate the interior of the new station on Cole Parkway, the historical society opened up its photo archives to the Coast Guard. The historical society, under the leadership of president and maritime history author David Ball, accepted the artifacts into the Scituate Maritime & Irish Mossing Museum's collection. Opening the door and stepping inside, the first thing one sees is the old floor mat of the Scituate station, emblazoned with a forty-four-foot motor lifeboat and the insignia of the station.

The museum is also home to many of the region's most significant maritime and search and rescue history artifacts. Several items from the steamer *Portland*, including doors, a life jacket and a butter dish, are interspersed with items from other wrecks in the Orientation and Shipwreck Rooms. Scituate also boasts one of the latest successful uses of the breeches buoy system, film footage of which can be seen in the *Etrusco* exhibit. The only major difference between that 1956 rescue and those of the Life-Saving Service era has to do with the method of shooting the projectile to the ship. By the 1950s, the Coast Guard had started using shoulder-fired line-throwing guns, an example of which is on display in the Lifesaving Room.

The Lifesaving Room is also home to several lifesaving medals given for rescues in town, Humane Society boat oars, a Hunt gun and a crowning centerpiece made from

The Manomet Point station, unfortunately, did not survive the wrecking ball's attack. *Courtesy of the National Archives and Records Administration.*

the wreckage of the brig *T. Remick*. According to the *Hull Beacon* of August 15, 1902, "H.C. Dimond of Boston presented Capt. [George] Brown a model of the James beach apparatus handcart, such as all life saving crews use, as a token of appreciation of the work of the crew. The model adorns the captains' room at the station and is constructed from copper bolts from the brig and wood from her cabin. On the top of the model's case is a bell presented by Capt. L.H. Forrest." The model, in all its minute detail, stands on its own pedestal in the museum.

While the Marshfield community certainly embraces its history, as evidenced through the Historic Winslow House, the Webster Estate, the Marcia Thomas House and the work of the Marshfield Historical Society, they have lost what could have been the Marshfield Maritime Museum. The town of Marshfield tried for ten years to wrestle the Brant Rock Life-Saving Station away from General Services Administration, but when the federal government finally signed it over to the town, the station was in such a bad state of decay it had to be torn down for safety reasons. The only other building standing in town that may have any connection to the Life-Saving Service era is 50 Cove Street, which, according to authors Cynthia H. Krusell and Betty Magoun Bates in *Marshfield: A Town of Villages*, may be an old Humane Society shelter. An open, stony lot, mirrored by the one on Fourth Cliff, stands where the Brant Rock station once did.

The Gurnet Point Life-Saving Station has fared much better. As with other lifesaving stations no longer deemed necessary for the needs of national defense, or of any other value to the federal government, the Gurnet Point station finally fell to auction to the general public. Seventy-three individuals expressed interest in purchasing the remote station, including Mr. Charles A. Brooks, the general manager of the Mystic Seaport

The boat room may be all that survives, attached to a house miles away. *Courtesy of the National Archives and Records Administration.*

Marine Historical Association, Inc. (Mystic later bought and moved the New Shoreham Life-Saving Station from Block Island, Rhode Island, for display at Mystic Seaport Museum); Congressman Hastings Keith; and Sydney W. Grossman of the Quincy-Grossman Surplus Company in Braintee, a lumber dealer. The high bid of $17,355 came in 1968 from Richard Boonisar of Wellesley Hills, who agreed to pay $347 quarterly for ten years to purchase the station. (At the same time, Pierre-Yves Cathou of Cambridge bid $24,500 to purchase the rest of the government's lands on the Gurnet, containing the old fort and lighthouse.) The Boonisar family still owns the station today, opening it annually for public viewing during the Duxbury Bay Maritime School's "Opening of the Bay" event.

The old bones of the *Venus*, wrecked on Saquish Beach during the Portland Gale, still reappear from time to time after the beach has been scoured by heavy storms, and to this day the boat room doors that troubled Keeper Rogers back in November 1898 still have trouble staying closed when a good burst of wind hits the area.

The Coast Guard declared the Manomet Point Life-Saving Station surplus on December 12, 1955, and the bids poured in, from Fair Lawn, Westfield and Union City, New Jersey; Darby and Philadelphia, Pennsylvania; Washington, D.C.; Hutchinson, Kansas; Scottsdale, Arizona; New York City, Brooklyn, Pelham and Niskayuna, New York; Dover and Wilmington, Delaware; Portsmouth and McLean, Virginia; South Bend, Indiana; Coronado, California; Haisdale, Illinois; Grand Rapids, Michigan; and Cambridge, Springfield, Somerville, Watertown, Shrewsbury, Attleboro and Hingham, Massachusetts (A.J. McEachern of 34 Emerald Street, Hingham, also attempted to buy the Brant Rock station). In the end, the station passed to Homer Arnold of Manomet.

The five-masted schooner *Nancy*, which came ashore on Nantasket Beach in a February 1927 storm, was the last hurrah for the South Shore's wooden lifeboat heroes. *Courtesy of the Hull Historical Society.*

The old Manomet Point boathouse has been moved from the beach and is now a private residence on Highland Terrace. All that remains of the Manomet Point story today is a small monument to the three surfmen who lost their lives in the *Robert E. Lee* tragedy of 1928. A lobster pound looks out over the bluff toward Mary Ann Rocks. Decaying ruins of the old launch way at the base of the cliff are exposed at low tide. While the main station building is gone, a portion of it may remain. Life-Saving Service historian Richard Boonisar, while driving northward on Route 3A from Cape Cod, swerved to the side of a road one day and recognized a familiar window pattern, and surmised that he might be looking at the exterior side wall of the Manomet Point boat room. It may be all that's left.

To say that that's all that's left of the Life-Saving Service era on the South Shore—a few monuments, artifacts, buildings and memories—would be denying the fact that the occupational descendants of the old surfmen and keepers, today's Coast Guardsmen and women, carry on the Life-Saving Service spirit. Their work lives, while made more efficient by radar, LORAN and eventually the global positioning system, more powerful and capable boats, better training, the invention of the helicopter and more, still mirror those days of the Life-Saving Service. They still watch the waters off the South Shore for mariners in distress, and still respond in the cold, the wind, the rain and the snow. The Coast Guard has even resurrected the name "surfman," giving it only to boat coxswains who pass rigorous heavy weather training at the service's National Motor Lifeboat School in Ilwaco, Washington.

As long as there is a Coast Guard presence on the South Shore, the spirit of the United States Life-Saving Service will live on.

BIBLIOGRAPHICAL ESSAY

The academic side of the history of the United States Life-Saving Service has gone through quite a growth spurt in recent years. As such, there is now a vast library of books on both the national story and the regional histories of the surfmen and keepers of yesteryear.

Several studies have become standards of the industry. Ralph Shanks, Lisa Woo Shanks and Wick York's *The United States Life-Saving Service: Heroes, Rescues and Architecture of the Early Coast Guard* (Petaluma, CA: Costano Books, 1996) is regarded as the bible, the quick reference tool, for any historian researching the history of the service. Dennis L. Noble's *That Others Might Live: The United States Life-Saving Service, 1878–1915* (Annapolis: Naval Institute Press, 1994) follows closely on its heels, while regional titles like Frederick Stonehouse's *Wreck Ashore: The United States Life-Saving Service on the Great Lakes* (Duluth, MN: Lakes Superior Port Cities, Inc., 1994), Van R. Field's *Wrecks & Rescues on Long Island: The Story of the U.S. Life Saving Service* (East Patchogue, NY: Searles Graphics, Inc. [the author], 1997) and Joe Mobley's *Ship Ashore: The U.S. Life-Savers of Coastal North Carolina* (Raleigh: North Carolina Division of Archives & History 1994) offer excellent introductory chapters on the formative years of the service. J.H. Merryman's *The United States Life-Saving Service—1880* (Golden, CO: Outbooks, 1981, reprint) is a short, readable snapshot of the service in those early years. The United States Life Saving Service's *Annual Report of the Operations of the United States Life-Saving Service 1875–1915* (Washington, D.C.: Government Printing Office, 1875–1915) are, as stated in the text, some of the best documents ever produced by our federal government, as far as readability goes. Wick York's unpublished master's of arts thesis "The Architecture of the United States Life-Saving Stations" (Boston University, 1983) is the standard work on the topic, bar none.

The most thorough books ever written on the early lifesaving equipment were done by Robert Bennett Forbes of the Humane Society of the Commonwealth of Massachusetts—*Lifeboats, Projectiles and Other Means for Saving Life* (Boston: W.M. Parsons Lunt, 1872)—and J. Paul Barnett, *The Lifesaving Guns of David Lyle* (Plymouth, IN: Town and Country Press, 1976).

The story of the 1840s and 1850s appropriations, and the role of William Augustus Newell in the founding of the Life-Saving Service, are found in Robert F. Bennett's *Surfboats, Rockets, & Carronades* (Washington, D.C.: Government Printing Office, 1976) and Reverend Lloyd R. Applegate's *A Life of Service: William Augustus Newell* (Toms River, NJ: Ocean County Historical Society, 1994). Margaret Thomas Buchholz's *New Jersey Shipwrecks: 350 Years in the Graveyard of the Atlantic* (Harvey Cedars, NJ: Down the Shore Publishing, 2004) highlights the stories of the shipwrecks in that state that led to the agitation for a federal lifesaving service.

The early history of shore-based lifesaving in Massachusetts, specifically the efforts of the Humane Society, is told best by Mark Anthony DeWolfe Howe's *The Humane Society of the Commonwealth of Massachusetts: An Historical Review 1785–1916* (Boston: Printed for the Humane Society at the Riverside Press, Cambridge 1918). Edouard Stackpole's *Life Saving Nantucket* (Nantucket: Stern-Majestic Press, Inc., 1972) also covers those early years. William A. Baker's *A History of the Boston Marine Society, 1742–1981* (Boston: Boston Marine Society, 1982) thoroughly details that organization's tale.

John W. Dalton's *The Life Savers of Cape Cod* (Boston: The Barta Press, Printers, 1902) is the book that this book is loosely based on. The nearly forty issues of *Wreck & Rescue Journal*, the quarterly magazine of the United States Life-Saving Service Heritage Association, and of which I'm proud to be editor, contain countless tales of Life-Saving Service and early Coast Guard. The association's first book *They Had to Go Out…True Stories of America's Coastal Life-Savers From the Pages of "Wreck & Rescue Journal"* (Gwinn, MI: Avery Color Studies, Inc., 2007) is a compilation of some of the best writing on the subject over the past decade.

Community histories of the South Shore towns form a special collection of books that must be referenced when researching the history of the Life-Saving Service. Hull histories begin with William M. Bergan's *Old Nantasket* (North Quincy, MA: Christopher Publishing House, 1968). I've had the pleasure of writing several books on the community, including *When Hull Freezes Over: Historic Winter Tales from the Massachusetts Shore* (Charleston, SC: The History Press, 2005), which covers the story of Joshua James and the Portland Gale. James is a subject of a small biography written by the general superintendent of the Life-Saving Service himself, Sumner Increase Kimball's *Joshua James, Life-Saver* (Boston: American Unitarian Association, 1909).

E. Victor Bigelow's *A Narrative History of Town of Cohasset, Massachusetts* (Cohasset, MA: Committee on Town History, 1898) carries tales of woe about the shipwreck situation off that coast, and Henry David Thoreau's *Cape Cod* (New York: W.W. Norton & Company, Inc., 1951, reprint) details the loss of the brig *St. John* in 1849.

Scituate may be the most prolific town on the South Shore. One of the most important works for the purposes of this book was David Ball and Fred Freitas's *Warnings Ignored! The Story of the Portland Gale, November 1898* (Scituate, MA: privately printed, 1995), just one of many books that the authors have compiled on the history of that community. This book led the way for the publication of Mason Philip Smith and Peter Dow Batchelder's *Four Short Blasts: The Gale of 1898 and the Loss of the Steamer* Portland. Together these books entail the best out there on the Portland Gale. Harvey Hunter Pratt penned an important small work, *The Harbor at Scituate, Massachusetts*, recently reprinted by the Scituate Historical

Society. Scituate also compiled commemorative histories for the 300th (1936) and 325th (1961) anniversaries, and the Chief Justice Cushing Chapter of the Daughters of the American Revolution pulled together *Old Scituate* in 1921, reprinted in 2000 by the DAR and the Scituate Historical Society. Vincent L. Wood's *Plum Island Recollections* (Newburyport, MA: Newburyport Press, Inc., 1995) is the story of what happened to surfman Thomas Maddock of Scituate after he left the South Shore. Margaret Cole Bonney's *Scituate's Sands of Time* (Scituate, MA: privately printed, 1994), a series of anecdotes about the town's past, is well complemented by Barbara Murphy's *Irish Mossers and Scituate Harbor Village* (Scituate, MA: privately printed, 1980), which reserves its back section for the stories of the lifesavers of the Fourth Cliff and North Scituate lifesaving stations.

Joseph Foster Merritt's *Anecdotes of North River and South Shore* (Rockland, MA: Rockland Standard Publishing Company, 1928) is an absolute treasure of local history, with short tales on numerous topics, including the effects of the Portland Gale of 1898 on the North River.

Marshfield's contributions come in three major tomes. First, Lysander Salmon Richards's *History of Marshfield* (Plymouth, MA: Memorial Press, 1901) tells of the growth of Brant Rock through the eyes of T.B. Blackman. Joseph C. Hagar's *Marshfield: The Autobiography of a Pilgrim Town* (Marshfield, MA, 1940) served as the town's tercentennial history. The *piece de resistance* for Marshfield, though, is Cynthia Hagar Krusell and Betty Magoun Bates's *Marshfield: A Town of Villages* (Marshfield Hills, MA: Historical Research Associates, 1990), a remarkable book that never seems to age, even nearly two decades removed from its publication.

Arcadia Publishing's *Images of America* pictorial histories offer quick snapshots of local history intended to help whet a novice historian's appetite. Most of the towns in the region have published them. *Hull and Nantasket Beach* (Charleston, SC: Arcadia, 1998) and *Then and Now: Hull and Nantasket Beach* (Charleston, SC: Arcadia, 2001) were team efforts of which I was proud to be a part. *Scituate* (Charleston, SC: Arcadia, 2000) was also team effort by David Ball, Fred Freitas, Carol Miles and myself, while *Then & Now: Scituate* (Charleston, SC: Arcadia, 2002) was a collaboration by David Corbin and me. *Marshfield* (Charleston, SC: Arcadia, 2007) was coauthored by Cynthia Hagar Krusell and me. Jim Baker, historian nonpareil, published *Plymouth* (Charleston, SC: Arcadia, 2002).

William H. Marnell's *Vacation Yesterdays of New England* (NY: Seabury Press, 1975) covers the history of vacationing on the South Shore of Boston, with a particular focus on the Marshfield and Scituate coastlines.

The new standard work on Duxbury Beach and the Gurnet is *The Duxbury Beach Book* (Duxbury, MA: Duxbury Beach Reservation, Inc., 2007). And although he's not a book, with his knowledge he might as well be; much of my knowledge of the Gurnet station came directly from the owner of the station himself, Richard Boonisar.

The National Archives and Records Administration Northeast Region branch in Waltham holds treasures. The daily reports of the six stations involved in this book can be found there, as can the wreck reports and the secret weapon, the General Services Administration's real property disposal records.

Regional and local newspapers, especially historic editions of the *Boston Globe* and the *Hull Beacon*, provide deep details of the lifesaving story on the South Shore.

Various other publications have been referred to and are cited in the text.

THE UNITED STATES LIFE-SAVING SERVICE HERITAGE ASSOCIATION

Just a little more than a decade ago, the country's leading Coast Guard historians—specifically those men and women interested in the story of the United States Life-Saving Service—gathered on the Cape Cod National Seashore to discuss the current status and future of the vanishing architecture, artifacts and, most importantly, history of the early Coast Guard. This meeting was brought into being by the foresight of the early staff of the Hull Lifesaving Museum. The task they collectively outlined seemed overwhelming: could they save a significant cultural resource on a national scale before it was lost forever? They decided that even if they couldn't do that, as, for instance, more than half of the lifesaving stations built in the Life-Saving Service years (1848–1915) had already disappeared, they would at least go down trying, and doing so together.

From that small grouping of historians, writers, National Park Service personnel and museum professionals came two fertile ideas. First, they would form a national nonprofit organization based in Massachusetts, the United States Life-Saving Service Heritage Association, to "preserve the stations, history, boats and equipment of the U.S. Life-Saving Service and U.S. Coast Guard." Second, they voted to create a quarterly publication, *Wreck & Rescue Journal*, to keep alive the stories of the surfmen and keepers that manned lifeboats, rigged breeches buoys and otherwise did whatever they could to save mariners in distress at sea.

But that was in 1995. So what happened?

Today the United States Life-Saving Service Heritage Association (USLSSHA) is stronger than ever, receiving Congressional recognition at its tenth annual meeting, held at the Sleeping Bear Dunes National Lakeshore in Leelanau County, Michigan, in 2005 for ten years of work in historic preservation and recognition from the United States Coast Guard in Cleveland, Ohio, in 2007. *Wreck & Rescue* is read in Coast Guard stations all over America and is sent across our northern border to Canada, overseas to readers in England and Australia and has even been carried by U.S. Coast Guard representatives to their equivalents in China. In ten years, the *Journal* has doubled in size from sixteen to thirty-two pages, allowing for more, longer scholarly articles about the history of search

and rescue operations in the United States and around the world. Some of the stories told in this book originally appeared in *Wreck & Rescue Journal*.

The story of the success of the U.S. Life-Saving Service Heritage Association does not end with the quarterly publication of *Wreck & Rescue Journal*. The true strength of the organization rests with its membership, men and women from around the country dedicated to keeping this history alive. Some are descendants of surfmen, some own old stations, some grew up in Coast Guard towns and still others are just drawn to the tales of bravery inherent in the Life-Saving Service story. Whatever the reasons, they share a common passion.

That passion is exercised—literally—each fall, when the members of the organization gather in a different historically rich area of the country to continue the discussion started at the first annual meeting: what can we do to save the lifesavers' stories? In twelve years' time, the members of USLSSHA have met on the Cape Cod National Seashore, on the Outer Banks of North Carolina and at Sleeping Bear Dunes. They've spent an extended weekend on Nantucket, in and around Bath and Portland, Maine, on Wisconsin's Door Peninsula, in southern New Jersey, at Marquette on Michigan's Upper Peninsula and at the mouth of the Columbia River in Astoria, Oregon.

During the 2001 meeting in Scituate, Massachusetts, attendees rode Coast Guard boats from Station Point Allerton to America's oldest light station, Boston Light. They've climbed the South Manitou Lighthouse in Lake Michigan and sailed West Grand Traverse Bay on the schooner *Madeline*. In New Jersey their heads spun as they reached the dizzying heights of Cape May Lighthouse and Atlantic City's Absecon Lighthouse. In the Pacific Northwest they've joined the Coast Guard on forty-seven-foot motor lifeboats on the Columbia River Bar, the most dangerous stretch of water in the world. They've met with active Coast Guardsmen and women at small boat stations on canals, lakeshores and seashores; witnessed rescue demonstrations by HH-65 Dolphin helicopters training with small boat crews; and marched in the footsteps of the surfmen who once walked America's shoreline, lanterns in hand, vigilantly searching the horizon for lives to save.

And the story will continue, as the surface has barely been scratched. There have been preservation successes and failures, but all along the way there has been a constant push to educate the public about the amazing stories of the Coast Guard's past. And the fact is, the history of the surfmen and keepers of old is rewritten on a daily basis, as today's Coast Guardsmen and women embody the spirit, ethics and courage that drove the lifesavers of yore to do the incredible work they did.

The traditional, unofficial motto of America's search and rescue professionals of the past was, "They had to go out, they did not have to come back." Today's lifesavers use *Semper Paratus*, or "Always Prepared," as their creed, but the effect is nearly the same. While they do the work they do, the members of the U.S. Life-Saving Service Heritage Association have also pledged to be prepared to react at a moment's notice to do whatever is necessary to carry the Coast Guard story forward into the future. Perhaps after reading this book, you'll be ready to join them.

The United States Life-Saving Service Heritage Association
PO Box 213
Hull, MA 02045
www.uslife-savingservice.org

Visit us at
www.historypress.net